Washington Irving's
The Legend of Sleepy Hollow

A Play in Two Acts

Christopher Cook

Bloomington, IN Milton Keynes, UK

authorHOUSE

AuthorHouse™
1663 Liberty Drive, Suite 200
Bloomington, IN 47403
www.authorhouse.com
Phone: 1-800-839-8640

AuthorHouse™ UK Ltd.
500 Avebury Boulevard
Central Milton Keynes, MK9 2BE
www.authorhouse.co.uk
Phone: 08001974150

First published by AuthorHouse 8/22/2012

ISBN: 978-1-4259-3428-6 (sc)
ISBN: 978-1-4259-3427-9 (hc)
ISBN: 978-1-4634-9983-9 (e)

Library of Congress Control Number: 2006904714

Printed in the United States of America
Bloomington, Indiana

Originally adapted in 2002 by Christopher Cook

CAUTION

SPECIAL NOTE

Anyone receiving permission to produce WASHINGTON IRVING'S THE LEGEND OF SLEEPY HOLLOW by Christopher Cook is required to give due authorship credit to the playwright as the sole and exclusive author of the play in all programs, posters, flyers, and any and all other promotional printing in connection with performances of the play. In all instances in which the title of the play appears for purposes of advertising, publicizing or otherwise exploiting the play and/or a production thereof; the name of the author must appear on a separate line, in which no other name appears, immediately beneath the title and in size of type equal to 50% of the largest letter used for the title of the play. No person, firm or entity may receive credit larger than that accorded the author.

ACKNOWLEDGEMENTS

An artist is only as good as the legions of souls who enable him to create. Lord knows I could never have done it all alone and there are close, personal angels too numerous to thank here, but I'll do the best I can by singling out those who've made the most significant contributions to this project: First and foremost, the hard-working people of River Alliance: Executive Director, Mike Dawson, for taking a chance with my delusions of grandeur. He possesses that rare and wonderful gift of being able to "make it happen" under the performing arts' most extreme shackles of adversity: politics and poverty. His business acumen has proven exemplary and in some strange fashion he and I make up a sort of two-headed P.T. Barnum. We both have a tendency to first tell the people what we think will lure them to an event and then second, figure out a way to make good on our promises. This is a method of capitalizing on sensationalism, but it always makes for an altogether more exciting "sideshow" atmosphere. And thanks to Mike, we *have* made good on our promises!

Anna Stalnaker, whose diligence always proves a formidable yin to my disorganized yang. Her patience and attention to detail is un-equaled and she deserves the requisite kudos for cleaning up after my incompetence. Matt Croxton, artist, photographer, designer, auteur in his own right, who designed promotional materials so slick and impressive that High Voltage Theatre had to work that much harder to live up to the flashy images on the poster. Kelly Renata, who came into the picture our second time out with River Alliance. Her calm exterior and professional demeanor speaks volumes about her character. She possesses a yeoman's work ethic and thanks to her incredible expertise in video production, High Voltage's *Sleepy Hollow* now has a fine TV commercial. Kelly also gets the "bitten tongue award" for putting up with my tempestuous tantrums. I thank Geah Pressgrove, PR person extraordinaire of Ferrillo and Associates, for getting the word out. I am forever indebted to the good people of Security Federal Bank, without whom we would not have had the ways and the means to build Sleepy Hollow and Tarry Town, New York on a bank of West Columbia. Security Federal Bank is one of those rare, nurturing corporations that understand the importance of providing for charities and communities contractor. Your words and actions challenged us to push further and further and see this dream come to fruition. The naysayer, after all, is the artist's arch-nemesis and chief motivator as well. You, therefore, helped this production get where it is today. The proof, as they say, is in the pudding and this has been evidenced by the thousands of fans who continue to gorge themselves silly upon this annual treat, year after year.

PRODUCTION HISTORY

THE LEGEND OF SLEEPY HOLLOW was originally produced by High Voltage Theatre in conjunction with Midlands Technical College in Columbia, South Carolina. Directed by the author, the play opened October 25, 2002.

THE LEGEND OF SLEEPY HOLLOW was subsequently reprised by High Voltage Theatre in conjunction with The River Alliance. Directed by the author, the play opened October 16, 2003 at the West Columbia Riverfront Amphitheatre in South Carolina.

THE LEGEND OF SLEEPY HOLLOW was remounted with Cook's original script in October of 2007, after a two-year hiatus. The show was stage managed by Meg Richards, carpentered by Clayton Ingram, lighting designed by Laura Anthony, and sound engineered by Elisa and Tom Harvey. Directed and produced by the author, the **2007** cast was as follows:

Ichabod Crane	Christopher Cook
Headless Horseman	Jerry Gobel
Diedrich Knickerbocker	Mike Lee
Katrina Van Tassel	Victoria Myers
Abraham Van Brunt	Joey Vasquez
Baltus Van Tassel	Mike Lee
Mrs. Van Tassel	Lara South
Hans Van Ripper	Patrick Williams
Mrs. Van Ripper	Amy Pederson
Yost Van Houten	Paul Covington
Judith Gardenier	Elizabeth Bridges
Mort Vanderghast	Bill Canaday
Mrs. Vedder	Susan Crosby
Parson Brouwer	Alfred Kerns
Peter Vanderdonk	Tony Moore
Starkenfaust	Joey Vasquez
Erik Van Bummel	Dillon Ingram
Vincent Van Halen	Daniel Fuerst
Jonathan Doolittle	Austin Gilbert
Kristina Van Ripper	Copeland Hanshaw
Hilda Martling	Jessica Yarborough
Adelaide Herrmann	Allie Yates
Bess LeRoy	Stephanie Addison

For Carolina and Valentina,
who have re-awakened the sleeping hollows
of my heart.

FROM PAGE TO STAGE

A History
Of the
High Voltage Theatre Production

It is with great excitement that I invite you to crack open the spine of this commemorative edition of Washington living's The Legend of Sleepy Hollow, a play in two acts! The published script you now hold in your hands came about as a result of painstaking efforts to preserve what has become a mainstay in the annals of a local, but professional theatre company in Columbia, South Carolina. High Voltage Theatre, the aforementioned ensemble, was originally formed to create a new and innovative approach to live performance in the capital city of the Palmetto state. Our mission is to challenge the medium of the art and fill a void in Midlands' theatre which has previously been under-served. We seek to push the proverbial envelope of tradition in the theatre by emphasizing a more stylized approach to performance, production, and story-telling through all major modes of physical expression, be it stage combat, creative movement, or dance. The road has been arduous. It has been rewarding. It is, as they say, a labor of love.

As a child, I was prone to getting as close as I possibly could to amusement park haunted houses without actually stepping foot inside. We called them "spook houses" or "ghost rides". I would creep up to the door of the strange contraption, moving ever so slowly, closing in my proximity, as though gradually wading deeper and deeper into the cold and murky waters of terror. I would stand, transfixed, rapt in complete fascination at the horrific murals painted upon the flat facade of the funhouse ride. These depictions were always a nightmarish melange of blood and guts, hell fires, and a macabre coterie of caverns, corpses, and creeps. They made the paintings of Hieronymus Bosch look like scenes from Sunday in the Park with George.

Femme fatales writhed naked on the ends of meat hooks, torch flames shot upwards completely singeing the scalps of innocent children, cauldrons of boiling hot oil bubbled furiously as the eternally damned, certain to be quick-fried to a crackly crisp, were tossed in by hooded henchmen. Devils wielded pitchforks, hills of skulls and bones were stacked up neatly in corners, and ghouls, crypt-crashers, and tomb terrors broke free from their terrestrial bonds. Yes, I was mesmerized, held captive by the promise of such horrors raging within the confines of the house.

And I was safe as long as I stayed put, several feet in front of the ticket person. I was out of harm's way, outside in the light of day. I was forever intrigued, however, at the idea that some day I might actually be brave enough to enter the proverbial mouth of hell. One day I would strap myself into the seat of one of the wheeled wagons that no doubt rolled brazen ticket-payers into the depths of despair and ultimately led them straight to a slow and painful demise. Yes, one day I just might go in. I just might have to check the whole thing out from the inside.

But for a while I would stay right where I was. Because to actually pay the price of admission and subject myself to these rides of absolute horror? I could never do it. That would be crossing the line and I dared not cross the line for fear of what I might discover. What if, for example, the images on the outside were nothing compared to what was going on the inside? What if I were to venture forth into the unknown, into the land of the dead and damned, never to return to my own hearth and home? What if the whole enterprise were a ruse to lure me into a torture chamber especially designed to facilitate my pain and eternal agony?

Needless to say, the day finally came when I found myself a reluctant patron of the dark ride. As it happened, my father all but dragged me kicking and screaming into the Haunted Mansion at Disney World.

The business my father was in provided for annual stockholders conventions. These were typically held in cities whose economies were fueled by attractions of some tourist value. As corny as these family outings may sound, I must admit, these trips were one of the great perks of my childhood. A few times we went to Orlando, Florida and while there we never missed an opportunity to go to Disney World. Since my proclivities towards haunted houses had made themselves quite apparent by this time, Dad was certain to insure that I saw the granddaddy of them all. It resided, of course at Disney.

And so we went. The moment we stepped inside the gates of the magic kingdom my anticipation grew with every footstep. I knew that ultimately we would come upon the spooky structure and there would be no turning back. As we made our way through the park, we eventually encountered the cemetery outside along the walkway of the house. Ancient tombstones and statues adorned the outer grounds and featured bad puns and humorous epitaphs carved into their stone faces. This gave us something to occupy our time as we cued up like lemmings waiting to dive into the proverbial waters of terror. Our turn came up soon enough. We found ourselves at the front stoop of the old house. And like a giant maw preparing to receive its prey, the central portals of the mansion opened, allowing us entry.

The moment our group darkened the massive doorways, we were led into a circular atrium and instructed to stand in the center of the floor, the "dead" center, to be exact. Once we'd maneuvered as directed, we turned around to find that the doors through which we had entered had vanished completely and were replaced by solid, bare walls. There was ostensibly no escape. Lightning flashed to reveal the shadow of a hanging corpse above our heads, swinging to and fro. And as soon as it appeared, the candles of cob-web laden chandeliers flickered, lamplights in nearby wall sconces went out, then on again, and as thunder outside crackled I prayed the lights would not go out entirely. When all at once the interior was again fully illuminated, the shadow disappeared. All of a sudden, the floor beneath us began to sink, or was it that the ceiling was ascending? Immediately, we found ourselves beside a strange and macabre sort of conveyor belt with what seemed a train-load of hundreds of empty coffin-like tortoise-shell seats. These were clearly for us, the fresh meat.

This, I knew, portended no good for us. If I'd thought that I'd have a successful escape out of the depths of what was sure to prove Satan's gut, I would've bolted for a door, a window, anything allowing passage into the world of light outside. But I was witness to the transformation of walls from Victorian wainscoting to a veritable fortress. The laws of natural physics clearly did not apply here. There was, as I'd remembered, no way out.

Dad pulled me into the berth, we sat, and my uncontrollable shivering began. I clutched the old man so firmly my nose was pressed deep into the pit of his arm. I clenched my eyes closed-tight, but then cracked them just enough to peer into the world of phantasmagoria that lay in wait for us. Tears strung down my cheeks and I winced to hear foreboding music seeping in from all corners. There was no question, our doom was quite thoughtfully planned out by the dark forces of the underworld.

The ghastly meat train began its journey. As we made our way down a darkened corridor, our seat suddenly turned a corner wherein we found ourselves at the upper balcony of a staircase. To the right was a grand ballroom of waltzing spirits and in a sustained state of levitation, in the center, a crystal ball. Within its confines was the head of a witch forecasting our miserable fate. And while somewhere deep inside I knew that all of this was make-believe and we were actually at the corner of the world's most famous amusement park, I may as well have been descending into the bowels of Hell. My fear transcended my reason.

Spectral images hovered and swirled above us in the air, lit candelabras wafted down hallways, shadows of things unseen frolicked upon the walls as lighting and thunder continued to play out a symphony of sight and sound. I found myself being more and more able to open my eyes and take in the macabre delights that old man Disney had dreamed up for his brave patrons. As we got further and further into the abyss, more inventive creatures made themselves known. Hitchhiking ghosts descended upon us and it seemed there was no way to keep them out of our "cars". We passed by a wall with large mirrors and upon seeing our reflection discovered we had been commandeered by a particularly large spectre. There were even statues and busts of souls long since dead singing and howling with delight as we drew ever nearer.

A longer corridor with grave sites on either side of us lay in wait and upon entering the hall, we were attacked by screaming banshees which leapt out at us from behind every tombstone. This was the most nerve-wracking part of the "visit". Long periods of atmospheric effects were one thing but when certain sections of the mansion were designed to startle, jerk and jolt it's riders, well that was something else altogether. The moments in this hallway were excruciating because we knew that at some point something was going to jump out and try to grab us and our anxiety increased with every foot as we never knew when nor where it would happen.

Then suddenly it was over. Almost as quickly as it had all begun, we were clearly on our way out. An impish little gypsy-like wraith paged the exit doorway. Doll-like and surreal, she spoke to us as if to give one final goodbye on behalf of all the supernatural beings encased within the chamber of horrors. I had emerged from my worst nightmares incarnate and what was more I had come out alive and unscathed! As I stood in the safety of the sunshine, I felt a sense of awe and even reverence for the mechanical wonder that had just turned me into a sniveling bowl of coward soup. I turned to the giant house and saluted. I had just played victim to what was surely the behemoth of haunted house rides!

And it was then that I vowed I would one day scare the pants off of others! I would do this not out of some sick means to get back at the world, but rather because I saw the fun in being shocked out of one's wits and then told, "Just kidding!" I began to understand that by our very nature, we love to be frightened, and then subsequently returned to our cozy little existences wherein vampires and werewolves are only fairy tale creatures. I was all too willing to provide the source of that fear. And so it was, this aficionado of the horror genre was born!

The coming about of this particular project was not unlike most in the course of plotting and planning for production in live theatre. It usually starts with inspiration, occasionally brings about exasperation, and invariable ends in a lot of perspiration. The learning curve is extraordinarily high when bringing a creation from its point of conception all the way to tangible reality. And nothing is so labor-intensive as putting on a major show. It of course starts with an idea.

Now, in order to understand how this thing began in the first place, it is first necessary to go back a few years to the inception of a fantasy that has grown to nearly

unmanageable proportions like the fused extremities of Frankenstein's monster. From the start, I had fallen in love with the darker themes and images prevalent in Irving' s novella. His Sleepy Hollow was a world in which reality was in a state of constant flirtation with fantasy and the macabre. The very idea that a rider without a head bandied about in order to avenge his own demise within an otherwise bucolic community of Christian folk fascinated and exhilarated me. I therefore wanted to have a more intimate knowledge with the story.

I wanted to know it inside and out. I read it over and over and over again. And each time I opened the cover and turned the pages, I found something that I'd not seen before. I took it upon myself to look tragic flaw. As is his proclivity with the aforementioned woodlands, Crane cannot resist the seductive allure of the very thing that frightens him most, tales from the dark side.

Ichabod Crane is also somewhat of an anti-hero. At story's opening, Irving lulls the reader into the false security that the pedagogue is a standard hero. He shows an interest in Katrina that at the outset appears genuine, albeit a little odd. But lurking beneath the veneer of Crane's strange charm is a desire for wealth, and a penchant for gluttony,

In the end, it is vulnerability in the schoolmaster that makes The Legend of Sleepy Hollow a horror story.

The pumpkin represents the fruits of an agrarian society, one founded upon its fundamental need for self-preservation among its members. The farmers in Irving's story are providers, not only of the staples but also the fertility of a community that must procreat in order to survive. Perhaps the author's hints that the headless Hessian carries a pumpkin in tow, speaks to the mocking nature of demons. Whatever the case, the deeper meanings and messages of horror within the story are what drove me to consider it as a stage play.

I ruminated on the possibilities of bringing Washington Irving's jewel to theatrical life. I spoke not a word of my fancies to anyone. I rolled the idea over and over in my mind until it had become my own little personal reality. I moved on to other projects, always knowing that at some point I would come back to this tale that haunted me so. In essence, I had stored away the idea in my head and heart until the proper opportunity presented itself.

I had read Washington Irving's novella many years ago and remembered having loved the animated Disney version featuring the vocal talents of Bing Crosby. In the 80's, a made-for-TV film version starring Jeff Goldblum was the first significant live-action offering of this strange tale. It usually played on Sunday afternoons in October. I loved its quaint, intimate feel of community and beautifully shot snowy woodlands scenes. Goldblum was appropriately quirky in his rendition of Ichabod Crane. It is a shame that this version is so difficult to come by today. Here's hoping it will find its way in the pantheon of offerings available on DVD.

In more recent years, The Hallmark Hall of Fame brought the story of the strange school teacher to the small screen with the perfectly-cast

Brent Carver in the lead. Carver gave a quieter, yet more pompous reading to the role. He is perhaps my favorite Crane to date. And then of course there was Tim Burton's overdone Hollywood treatment starring the miss-cast Johnny Depp. I bought my ticket the first day the film came out eagerly awaiting the presentation of Lrving's tale on the big screen. While I didn't care for the liberties taken with the original story line, I was so incredibly blown away by the beautiful images and spectacular effects. It was, to say the least, awe-inspiring. Years later, I hadn't lost the excitement over what would later become my all-time favorite ghost story. I'd often wondered if Irving's story would work in the medium of live theatre.

Live theatre is immediate. It is an ephemeral If ever I were to produce the tale for the stage, I reasoned, I would first have to do my homework. I needed to know if there was a play version of the story. After a period of several months' research, I discovered that there were nearly no respectable stage adaptations of The Legend of Sleepy Hollow available. I felt that it was time for a full-fledged telling of the story, from beginning to end, a play that would encompass at least two acts with a healthy intermission betwixt. I'd also decided the show should be geared toward adults, be performed by adults and feature some of the most startling moments of horror placed onstage since the golden age of grand guinol. But I just wasn't ready yet to take on the rigors of mounting such a monolith of a piece. The time had to be right. The place had to be right.

On a late ride after a long rehearsal for a production of Othello, in which I was directing, I had given my friend, Reggie a lift home. On the way to his house, we engaged in one of many inspired conversations which turn into brain-storming sessions on what we'd like to see one day on stage, and more often than not, lapsing into digression on projects that we ourselves would like to do together in the theatre. We tossed back and forth a litany of ideas for productions and the spark of inspiration quickly turned to creative fire. The thoughts came quicker than we were able to voice them. Suddenly, Reggie got a gleam in his eye, turned to me and said, "You know what would make a cool stage play someday?" "What's that?". I responded. "The Legend of Sleepy Hollow!", he blurted with great enthusiasm.

I couldn't believe it. I nearly slammed on the brakes and sent us both flying into the windshield.

"You know something? I've always thought the same thing!" I exclaimed. We then brainstormed on how such a fantastical story could be made a reality.

Having been greatly inspired by the work of Julia Taymor, and her visionary works using over-sized masks, I suggested that similar methods of artistry could be used to create the more challenging of characters in the production. Perhaps the headless Hessian and his equine partner could be depicted through giant puppets. Eventually, I gave up the concept due to a lack of resources and financial feasibility. Puppets I would have to construct. Human actors I could get.

But where to find the script? That was the next great challenge. A production is only as good as the printed words which form the structure, content, and messages

As I'd previously mentioned, my subsequent research proved disappointing. I discovered only two published attempts at dramatizing the classic: I unearthed an antiquated musical from the early 1960s, and what amounted to nothing more than a one-act version intended for children that appeared to have been penned to accommodate touring theatre. Both versions were bereft of Washington Irving's more potent words. And the midnight ride of the "Headless Horseman" was reduced to a brief appearance in which no clear stage directions were given in order to clue the director in on how the effect was to be achieved indoors. Would an actor wear an over-sized coat over his head and hop around with a horse's mane on the end of a stick? Would two unfortunate souls squeeze themselves in to a horse costume, one at the head, the other at the posterior, crammed into the backside of the actor in front, ala Sondheim's Gypsy?

There had to be a way of bringing this marvelous and haunting yarn to the live stage without losing any of its integrity or imagery and flavorful language in the process. There had to be a way to preserve the venerable and well-known American tale. I envisioned a frilly-costumed, completely-propped, elegantly-lit, and fast-paced entertainment that would innovations of special effects which would enhance and serve the action onstage. Clearly the story was not written with a live production in mind as There is no quoted dialogue whatsoever, save for Ichabod

Crane's thought to make it to the bridge for safety. Also, the entire piece is structured as a narrative told by a single voice, that of Dietrich Knickerbocker. Besides the obvious principle players, who would be the other characters and from where would their names come? I needed to create the feel of an entire town, a community that is a healthy population. I went back to the novella and focused upon I then began reading Irving's other works including Rip Van Winkle.

One thing was sure, I was bound to "discover" the villagers' characters somewhere. Irving's other Hudson-area tales would certainly provide the I believed that while the original story is technically a novella, the staged presentation would play best in grand epic form. I also didn't see the story as a play for kids, although it should certainly be palatable for family audiences, while other moments needed to be appropriately dark and disturbing. I felt that an authentic telling of the legend required not only those tangible images that Irving provided, but also a personification of the demons lurking within the imaginations of the inhabitants, most especially those of Ichabod Crane.

In the early fall of 2002, I was an adjunct instructor of Theatre at Midlands Technical College in Columbia, South Carolina. I taught an Acting 105 course to a cozy little group of five students who were enrolled. As it happened, we were all at that point in the semester getting rather bored. Desperate to find something which would excite the imagination of the class, I offered that we put together a little presentation of a play which would be edgy yet appropriate for the public at large. When I suggested Washington Irving's timeless classic The Legend of Sleepy Hollow, The student's moods had changed. Eyes opened wide and mouths dropped agape. Immediately, the enthusiasm in the 90-seat auditorium was palpable and the project took off. It had only been a few years since Burton's film hit the cinemas and became the non-reading public's only access to Irving's legend. Burton certainly captured the imagination of the average movie-goer, but what I wanted to do was bring to the stage a more authentic and reverent telling to the tale. I was certainly fueled by Burton's treatment, the atmosphere he created and his penchant for gothic horror. Yet what, I wondered, would happen if one were to adapt the story using the imaginative reminiscent of Burton's visionary world and blend those elements with Irving's original storyline, language and themes.

The following day my lesson plans focused on the techniques and processes of stage reading. The criteria of which included careful attention to pronunciation, enunciation, articulation, and vocal production. It gave the students an opportunity to apply the basic tenets of acting to the reading of an American classic. I thought it valuable to simply listen to the story being told by college students, young voices with an obvious enthusiasm for the project. It worked! What the students lacked in technical reading skills they more than made up for in chutzpa. This was the test I needed to evaluate the feasibility of what we were attempting to do.

We sat in a circle on stage the six of us, simply taking turns reading aloud from the novella. Each student took a paragraph and we just alternated this way until the whole thing was finished. It took us about two class periods to complete just this phase. We knew we liked the story but we all agreed that it would be quite a challenge to put the thing on. After all, as was previously stated, there was virtually no dialogue in Irving's tale that we could pull from the pages and lay out into a script format. Also, the students were having trouble with some of the language, as Irving's vocabulary can at times prove rather daunting.

It was decided that I would spend the weekend seeing what could be done with the story. I went home that Friday and set to work. I re-read the story over and over, jotting down notes and ideas along the margins. I studied and kept a dictionary nearby as reference for the more arcane vocabulary that I was not using in my daily life.

Then began the arduous task of taking the prose piece and adapting it into play form. I started by taking an inventory of the characters in Irving's story. There really weren't many to start with. This is perhaps why I thought it might make a nice play for five students.

It took only a weekend, a ream of typing paper and bottomless cups of coffee and I had come through on my promise. We had a play. A short one and one that needed development, but we had a play nonetheless. And all six of my students had parts. I brought in a couple of outside performers from the community to round out the cast and we were ready to go! Rehearsals sailed along, we borrowed costumes from the local Shakespeare company, and invited the public free-of -charge to come see our little play. The truth is, by that time in my career I had already amassed quite a professional resume with credits from regional theatres ranging from New York to Chicago to San Francisco. But virtually nothing that I had done previously was as exciting to me as the afternoon we opened The Legend of Sleepy Hollow.

With more gumption than resources, my students and I had proven that sometimes all one needs is belief and effort. And these were the two ingredients in great supply I'd spent no more than $100 on the production. We offered it to the public for free. As I was also teaching Theatre and Speech at Newberry College at the time, I decided to bring the show to the students there as part of a cultural requirement fulfillment offering. Subsequently, the student body at Newbeny was treated to our play on a cool and crisp Halloween afternoon. We brought the production back to Midlands Tech for a final weekend of performances. On word of mouth alone, by the end of the short run, nearly 300 people had turned out to see the quiet little play in 2002. We were off to an auspicious beginning!

Determined to keep the production alive as well as to pursue the dream of turning it into an epic-scale outdoor production, I searched out alternative theatres in which the play could be performed. Someone had told me the previous year about the existence of a newly-built amphitheatre just across the Gervais Street bridge in West Columbia. I thought that if it is true this could be my golden opportunity. I decided to check it out.

On a warm and rainy afternoon in April, I threw on an old raincoat and hat, packed a sandwich, a cup of coffee and my favorite Todd Rundgren CD then got behind the wheel of my Honda Civic. I took a drive across town heading toward West Columbia. When I'd reached the Gervais Street Bridge, I could just make out the edge of what appeared to be a slight clearing to the left of the bridge.

Lo and behold, it was true! There was the amphitheatre that only minutes ago, as far as I was concerned, was simply a rumor. There were seven levels of stone seating which descended upon a muddy puddle-filled "stage" and beyond the foliage, the vast and majestic Congaree River. It was nearly to good to be true.

Having no clue who to speak to about securing the theatre for the production, I finally got in touch with a man by the name of Mike Dawson at the River Alliance. I told him I had a vision for a grand-scale period outdoor spectacle that would be appropriate for families and the central community at large and that I felt that the West Columbia Riverwalk Amphitheatre would be the perfect venue for such an event. He was intrigued with the idea and said he'd give me a meeting. We sat down to discuss the project over coffee. I'd brought in the couple of press clippings I'd had on the 2002 production and did my best to pitch the idea to him as though I had an unlimited budget and what doing something of this size and scale would require. We didn't really have the money but that I knew that we could be resourceful enough to see the dream come to fruition. He suggested we approach several local corporations and seek funding in order to bank some starter capital.

We approached Security Federal Bank with our proposal and they graciously agreed to make a donation to our cause. Now, with the support of the corporate community and a little cash in our pocket, we could begin envisioning the show for outdoors. We made several enhancements in order to best serve the play for our new venue and a hopefully growing audience. The demands of the medium of outdoor drama' dictated that everything be blown up to a size proportionate to the expectations of viewers who would be sitting on stone steps and sharing an experience in a natural environment.

We therefore added several elements to the production to give it a bigger, more epic look. We brought in professional equestrians in order that the headless horseman would be an actor riding a living horse. We rented a professionally-constructed costume with built-up shoulders and a stiff collar and cape, giving the Hessian a more realistic appearance. The rental fee was expensive and the costume not quite 1700's period, but it was more functional than the blow-up plastic model from last year.

We built an exterior set: a church, a livery stable, a well-to-do farmer's home, and an Inn. We increased the cast number from seven to thirteen, we added a swordfight, a period dance, a live chorus, and a legion of walking corpses. The size of our performance space lent itself to greater possibilities for movement across the stage and the house, of course, accommodated some two hundred more patrons than did the lecture hall at Midlands Tech.

Rehearsals went smoothly, tech week was relatively painless, and opening night was a grand success! We had filled nearly every seat in the amphitheatre and played to an audience that included city and state officials, the mayor of West Columbia and the local press. At intermission we sold hot apple cider, hot chocolate, cold beverages and cookies. When the curtain came down, families were invited to come back stage and have their pictures taken with the headless Hessian and his horse. The following week, the reviews were in the papers and High Voltage Theatre's The Legend of Sleepy Hollow was an official smash hit. By closing night of the play, we were selling to capacity and actually had to turn people away for lack of seating accommodations. It was a great problem to have! The 2003 season couldn't have gone any better!

2004 marked an exciting turning point for the production. We had been invited back! We had again been offered carte blanche at the West Columbia Riverwalk Amphitheatre. Sleepy Hollow on the River had officially become an annual event in the wilds of West Columbia. Now, with a little more capital banked than we had the year before, we decided to step-up the production values of our growing magnum opus. We went from last year's rented and much over-priced Headless Horseman costume, to a rig built specifically to fit the frame of our equestrian-actor, Jerry Gobel. His head and neck were more comfortable, he had better control of vision, and we had costumed the contraption to appear more 1700's Hessian. Most importantly, we now owned the costume! We could eliminate rental charges as a compulsory line-item in our overhead.

The set also took a gigantic leap forward and upward with the hiring of cracker-jack scenic designer Charles Whetzel. Early on, Mr. Whetzel and I scheduled meetings in which we explored the most reasonable ways to fulfill my vision of an 18th - Century Dutch farming village at the amphitheatre. We studied video, we thumbed through books, we perused photos,, we surveyed paintings, etc. Charles feverishly sketched out renderings as we brainstormed the designs of everything from dormer windows to bi-level stables. His drawings were imaginative and truly captured the feel of the story and its locale. In the end, with the assistance of carpenter Paul Pabst, Charles Whetzel had designed and built an impressive and functional world for our play.

George Mirabel's lighting design was also a welcome innovation for the '04 production. The previous year we had sort of fumbled around with lighting, making sure we could at least see our actors and then using a "special" here or there to provide the obligatory moment of supernatural atmosphere. But now we had commissioned a professional to shed some real light upon our stage. George had made magic with his instruments: morning sun bathed our characters in warmth for the crack of dawn scenes, the 'walking dead' emerged from ghastly blue pools of light, the headless horseman galloped out of moonlit rays stenciled by the shadows of creeping branches. It was more than any director could hope for.

The wonderful thing about an annual event of this type is that it can grow from year to year. While we did not have the funding to completely fulfill my vision for this show our first time out of the gate, I knew that we could start off small and gradually add to the production values. The sky as they say truly is the limit and we are only as restricted as our imaginations allow us to be.

Each year we were able to build onto the production. There was an exponential increase in our resources due to the growing number of patrons who made their way to the Riverwalk Amphitheatre in a curious pilgrimage to see what all the hoopla was about. As the show became more popular and seen by hundreds more each season, the coffers gradually grew larger Some ninety percent of these profits put back into the production in order to bring to the public a bigger and better show each Halloween.

Proceeds from the play also provided for charites such as the Lou Holtz Homeless Shelter, WA Perry Middle School, and the children of St. Lawrence Place, a transitional housing facility for lower income families.

And so it was, with costume, set, and lighting designs all receiving a much-needed over-hall, word got out that the '04 production was the best ever. Within a year, attendance to the production seemed to triple. High Voltage Theatre's The Legend of Sleepy Hollow had now reached its zenith. We had yet a third year of success under our belt!

Today, The Legend of Sleepy Hollow is a bona-fide annual tradition in these parts. Far has it come from the ninety-seat lecture hall at Midlands Tech, a budget of a hundred bucks, and a headless horseman with inflatable plastic shoulders from the bargain bin costumes at Party City. In the beginning, River Alliance and High Voltage Theatre became a formidable partnership and were devoted to keeping the stage play alive. We have since gone our separate ways. Others will come and go and will carry the torch for as long as they see fit. My sincere hope is that Washington Irving's story will remain un-besmirched by errant and unnecessary controversy.

As far as High Voltage Theatre is concerned, it seems we struggle every year as the dreams grow larger and the money grows shorter. Such is the nature of the not-for-profit arts. But there's more to keeping a fantasy fulfilled than filthy lucre. It takes dedicated and hard-working volunteers who believe in a project and pour their own blood, sweat, and tears into the daily minutiae that is "putting on a play". Where there is hope, there is always a possibility.

In the end, when the fog has cleared, the lights gone down, music faded, the actors gone home, and the horses put to stable, all that remains is the drive home for the family who came to share with us in the magic of oral tradition. Whether we are performing outdoors in a Grecian amphitheatre or in a cramped and sweaty lab-theatre, we will always give it our all and we hope that there will be more returnees each subsequent season.

If someone had told me several years ago that the little one-hour play I adapted from Irving's quaint piece of Americana, would one day balloon into an albeit local cultural phenomenon, to quote Annie Wilkes from Stephen King's MISERY, "I would've checked both legs to see which one was being pulled!" But we made it happen. And not only did it happen, but it yielded commercial success a hundred fold. The simple truth is that the project exceeded my wildest dreams. It has become, for me, validation of years and service to the American stage. And if for nothing else than the sake of being able to claim ownership of the first three years of production, it has been well worth it.

I remember that at the tender age of about twelve, I asked my father if, when I grew up I could have an amusement park of my own. Our production of The Legend of Sleepy Hollow was just that. It created a time and place where people could go every year to escape the doldrums of daily life only to leap into a world of horror fantasy. Our audiences were lulled into a false sense of comfort, and then ultimately scared out of their wits. The scripted play you now hold has all the crests and dips of a roller-coaster ride and more costumes than the strolling street players of a Renaissance faire. Our productions in the early part of this century, based on this script, were proof positive that theatre can continue to grow and push the bounds of its definition.

Theatre can be anything we want it to be. It can transpire, transgress, and transcend that of all other art forms because its inherent nature is to continue to develop, mutate, and morph in order to facilitate the desires of what its society needs to express. On the other hand, by definition theatre has only three requirements: material (that is to say, a script of some sort), actors to present said material, and an audience. This is theatre in its purest form. This is what we seek to explore.

Live theatre laden with technological gimmickry such as video projection and surround-sound for example, may be a current fad but at day's end, it will prove "full of sound and fury, signifying nothing". Pure theatre needs no help. Digital imagery and laser light shows are nothing to the point. In the end, what the audience takes with them is drama, a well-told story of conflict between and among those of us who share in this thing we call humanity. I was taught by many a professor in grad school, "Have good material. Present it as best you can." The Legend of Sleepy Hollow is of the best of material. It needs only the cogent directing and superior acting that comes with expertise.

And thus it is with any literary piece of national treasure. We should always strive to produce stage plays with standards concomitant with the quality of the written word. We owe it to the authors. There are a lot of great stories out there. The best ones accurately reflect humankind's vast array of strengths and foibles and how these characteristics play themselves out in a world rife with temptation, mystery, humor, light and darkness. Washington Irving's novella is just one example of so many tales of "gothic horror" which paint with words a rich tapestry depicting a landscape of a by-gone era we all desire to have experienced.

The credit, therefore, for the commercial success of any telling of The Legend of Sleepy Hollow, be it stage, film, TV or radio, ultimately lies not in the playwright, producer, director, nor actors, but rather in the author of the original spooky tale. That brave and brilliant man who first dipped quill into the wellspring of imagination and painted a portrait of American life as sentimental as a painting by Wyeth and as inherently indigenous to our landscape as a symphony by Copeland.

We who bring such stories to the masses by way of mediums other than those for which their originators intended, are merely enablers.

We are interpreters who through our individual crafts give voice to text. In the case of The Legend of Sleepy Hollow, I know this to be true. In spite of all that has happened, I am forever grateful for the opportunities I've had to inhabit Tarry Town and I wouldn't trade a minute of the experience for anything in the world. In the end, I am not so much an interpreter, but rather a humble servant who has attempted to take what has become an icon of American literature and breathe into it, new life. My only hope is that Mr. Irving may forgive my hubris.

Christopher Cook

Columbia, SC

2007

"I know who the Dead Ones are.
They are the guests
of the Human Community
who are neighbors to us
of the forest."

-Wole Soyinka
A Dance of the Forests

DRAMATIS PERSONAE

Ichabod Crane, an odd schoolmaster, new to Sleepy Hollow.

Katrina Van Tassel, Baltus' coquettish daughter, eighteen or so.

Diedrich Knickerbocker, a venerable storyteller who bears a striking resemblance to Washington Irving.

Abraham Van Brunt, aka "Brom Bones", handsome, young, rival suitor to Katrina.

Baltus Van Tassel, A prosperous farmer, devoted father and husband.

Mrs. Van Tassel, Baltus' wife and devoted mother to Katrina.

Hans Van Ripper, Horse breeder and neighbor to the Van Tassels.

Mrs. Van Ripper, Hans' wife, and friend to the Van Tassels.

Kristina Van Ripper, young daughter to the Van Rippers.

Peter Vanderdonk, a messenger to the Van Tassel house.

Doffue Martling, a large, blue-bearded Dutchman. A jolly war storyteller.

Judith Gardenier, purveyor of produce, opportunist, and daughter to legendary Rip Van Winkle,

Nicholas Vedder, a reticent inn-keeper.

Mrs. Vedder, Nicholas' wife and partner in family business.

Yost Van Houten, an eccentric architect.

Hilda Martling, Doffue's wife, purveyor of meats and baked goods.

Derrick Van Bummel, friend to Brom Bones.

Jonathan Doolittle, friend to Brom Bones and Derrick Van Bummel.

Headless Horseman, the supposed spectre of a slain Hessian trooper.

Sleepy Hollow Boy, an "unclaimed" urchin of town, the young Knickerbocker.

BREAKDOWN OF SCENES

ACT I

ACT II

Washington Irving's

The Legend of Sleepy Hollow

A Play in Two Acts

Christopher Cook

ACT I

PROLOGUE

(Autumn, 1795. It is a valley near the banks of the Hudson River in the upstate of New York. The play opens as an appropriate moment in pre-show music gives way to the darkening of the house and an eerie supernatural light rising upon the stage. Soft, mysterious music, orchestral and ghostly in nature, fills the air as fog creeps in. Light reveals a tree in the background center. It is tall and gnarled with twisted branches that reach out menacingly like the arms of an old witch. It is the tree upon which Major Andre, a revolutionary war officer was hanged for treason. The entire set is a beautiful and haunting representation of a small Dutch village. Geoffrey Crayon, a writer, appears, lights his clay pipe, and speaks.)

CRAYON

Our story begins in a little valley, or rather lap of land, among high hills, by the name of Sleepy Hollow. The whole neighborhood abounds with local tales, haunted spots and twilight superstitions. The dominant spirit, however, that haunts this enchanted region, and seems to be commander-in-chief of all the powers of the air, is the apparition of a figure on horseback without a head. It is said by some to be the ghost of a Hessian trooper whose head had been chopped cleanly off during the summer of 1776, when the British undertook their first major offensive in New York in the battle that sparked the Revolutionary War.

Scene 1. "The Battle"

(A canon explodes. Muskets fire. War music blares. Wounded Patriot soldiers appear and take cover to ambush advancing Red Coats. Red Coats enter with Hessian trooper. The fighting range gets closer and closer as weapons move from muskets to muskets and bayonets to saber swords and hand-to-hand. The Hessian begins killing everyone in his wake. He is finally overtaken by Patriots who hold him down, draw a saber, and lop off his head. Several British soldiers retreat as they witness their comrades getting killed. The Hessian's severed head, streaming blood, is lifted in triumph, the decapitated corpse is dragged off into the woods, the cheers of revolutionaries follow as all retreat, smoke clears.)

Scene 2. "Dutch Settlers"

(Gentler music fades in with lighting to reveal Knickerbocker at an old writing desk in the corner of a cozy little loft in the Van Ripper's Barn. A distinguished man in what appears to be his mid to late sixties, he has a commanding presence and speaks with the heir of a man who has lived long enough to have told his fare share of folk tales. He pulls out a quill and opens a journal. He strikes a match to light an oil lamp nearby and then his long-stemmed pipe. The light level intensifies as if conjured by some magical power. Knickerbocker blows a smoke ring, and begins writing his story as he addresses the audience. Music should gently underscore most of his monologue. Inhabitants of Sleepy Hollow gradually enter to do daily chores in their respective homes and gardens. Eventually, the entire stage is filled with villagers moving in slow motion.)

<u>KNICKERBOCKER</u>

In the bosom of one of those spacious coves that indent the eastern shore of the Hudson River lies a small market port by the name of Tarry Town. Not far from this village, there is a little valley, which is one of the quietest places in the whole world. A small brook glides

3

through it, with just murmur enough to lull one to repose, and the occasional whistle of a quail, or tapping of a woodpecker, is almost the only sound that ever breaks in upon the uniform tranquility. I recollect that when a stripling, my first exploit in squirrel shooting was in a grove of tall walnut trees that shades one side of the valley. *(Enter boy as young Knickerbocker with a gun almost twice his size.)* I had wandered into it at noontime, when all nature is peculiarly quiet, and was startled by the roar of my own gun, as it broke the Sabbath stillness around and was prolonged and reverberated by the angry echoes. *(There is a shot. At this a few townspeople run to the boy to congratulate him on his kill. The villagers slowly exit.)* From the listless repose of the place, and the peculiar character of its inhabitants, who are descendants from the original Dutch settlers, a drowsy, dreamy influence seems to hang over the land, and to pervade the very atmosphere. *(Enter Sleepy Hollow Boys)* Its rustic lads, Brom Bones, Derrick Van Bummel and Jonathan Doolittle are called the Sleepy Hollow Boys throughout all the neighboring country.

Scene 3. "Living Scarecrow"

KNICKERBOCKER

Now, in this by-place of nature there abode, in a remote period of American history, that is to say, some thirty years since, a worthy weight by the name of Ichabod Crane.

(Ichabod Crane enters with a long staff balanced over one shoulder and all his worldly possessions tied up in a cloth on one side of it. He also carries a small stack of books bound by twine.)

KNICKERBOCKER

He sojourned, or, as he expressed it, "tarried", in Sleepy Hollow for the purpose of instructing the children of the vicinity. He was tall, but exceedingly lank, with narrow shoulders, long arms and legs and hands that dangled a mile out of his sleeves. Upon the stranger's arrival emerged from the wood a most enthusiastic or shall I say, "appreciative" welcoming committee.

(Knickerbocker exits. As Ichabod sits upon a stump to wipe his weary brow, the Sleepy Hollow Boys approach)

VAN BRUNT

Do my eyes deceive me?! It appears to be a living scarecrow eloped from a cornfield!

VAN BUMMEL

I think it's a corpse from the churchyard in search of a good meal.

VAN BRUNT

What do *you* say, Boy?

DOOLITTLE

It's a ghost! Can't you see his skin white as a sheet?

ICHABOD

My dear fellow!

VAN BUMMEL

It speaks!

ICHABOD

Well of course I speak. I am of the fortunate yet, sadly, few who can boast of being fully literate. I speak English, Latin, German, Italian, French, as well as your native Dutch....

VAN BUMMEL

And from whence do you hail, stranger?

ICHABOD

I am a native of Connecticut.

DOOLITTLE

A Yankee!

VAN BRUNT

Connecticut!

ICHABOD

Careful, careful. It is a state which supplies the Union with pioneers for the mind as well as for the forest, and send forth yearly its legions of frontier woodsmen and country schoolmasters.

VAN BUMMEL

The scarecrow is a state publicist to boot!

ICHABOD

Ichabod Crane, Pedagogue.

VAN BRUNT

Crane? Of course, a CRANE!!! ...Look, lads, we've got a giant foul on our stump!

(The boys do their best bird imitations.)

ICHABOD

Now, see here!

VAN BUMMEL

A crane, a crane!

VAN BRUNT

Come now, sir. Do you not admit your name is rather fitting?

ICHABOD

I concur the cognomen of my surname is not inapplicable to my idiosyncratic corpus.

VAN BRUNT

I can't tell whether he agreed with me or not?

VAN BUMMEL

Indeed the strange bird speaks a language not our own. I see his beak moving but I can't understand a word he's chirping!

VAN BRUNT

A rare breed! Derrick, take notes!

(Van Bummel pulls out a piece of parchment and a quill and begins writing down all that Brom Bones dictates.)

VAN BRUNT

We may have an endangered species on our hands! A Talking Crane! And foreign-tongued at that!

VAN BUMMEL

All right then, dear Doctor Bones, please dictate.

VAN BRUNT

Upon closer examination, the subject's frame is most loosely held together by dangling wings, stalky legs, and feet that may as well serve as shovels. His head is small, and flat at top, with huge ears, large green glassy eyes, and a long snipe nose,…

VAN BUMMEL

Is that a nose or a beak?

VAN BRUNT

Not sure. Perhaps it's a weathercrock, perched upon his spindle neck, to tell which way the wind blows. To see him striding along the profile of a hill on a windy day, with his clothes bagging and fluttering about him, one might mistake him for the genus of famine descending upon the earth!

7

(The boys break out into hysterical laughter and begin flapping their own wings, cawing and "flying" in a circle around Ichabod. Yost Van Houten enters. He is an eccentric architect whose apparel tells the story of a man more obsessed with his work than his dress. He sees what is happening and saves Ichabod Crane.)

VAN HOUTEN

Alright, you vagabonds! Enough! Enough! Let the poor man alone! Away with you!

(The boys run off mocking Crane, each with a stick on his shoulder and a handkerchief to his brow. The walks are exaggerated and grotesque. They explode into laughter as they exit. Yost Van Houten approaches.)

Scene 4. "Ichabod Meets Van Houten"

VAN HOUTEN

Pay them no mind. There's more mischief than ill will in their composition.

ICHABOD

Pardon, Myneer. But, I'm looking for the schoolhouse. You see, I'm the new schoolmaster and I understand the facility is somewhere nearby. Do you know it?

VAN HOUTEN

Know it, my good man? I designed it.

(He extends his hand. Ichabod shakes it.)

Yost Van Houten, Architect.

ICHABOD

Ichabod Crane, Pedagogue.

VAN HOUTEN

A pleasure. A pleasure. Now, the schoolhouse is a low building of one large room, rudely constructed of logs; the windows partly glazed, and partly patched with leaves of old copy books.

ICHABOD

Oh, my. It sounds rather Spartan. You see, I have many books that I'd hoped to store there. Is the schoolhouse secure?

VAN HOUTEN

It is most ingeniously secured at vacant hours, by a withe twisted in the handle of the door, and stakes set against the window shutters; so that though a thief might get in with perfect ease, he will find some embarrassment in getting out. An idea I borrowed from the mystery of an eelpot.

ICHABOD

Well, that should be sufficient. And how do I find it?

VAN HOUTEN

Follow this road apiece until you come to a clearing. The schoolhouse stands in a rather lonely but pleasant situation, just at the foot of a woody hill. You'll see a brook running close by, and a formidable birch tree growing at one end of it.

ICHABOD

Thank you, Myneer.

VAN HOUTEN

My pleasure…Oh, and if you should happen to need services of an architectural nature, here's my card. I can provide specs, renderings, and plans at no charge.

ICHABOD

Thank you, Myneer. I'll keep that in mind.

(A final handshake and Van Houten exits. Crane "enters" the schoolhouse.)

KNICKERBOCKER

Ichabod found the birchtree and the schoolhouse. As time passed and days turned into weeks, the Yankee schoolmaster settled into a comfortable routine. At the end of a crisp autumn school day, Ichabod Crane was known to remind his students that the birch tree was not only a thing of beauty, but also served for utilitarian purposes as well.

Scene 5. "Class Dismissed"

(He exits. Crane addresses the members of the audience as they become his students. He threateningly wields the birch switch for emphasis.)

ICHABOD

Pupils! As you've just been witness to the administering of justice at the expense of Master Van Rotten, the birch tree outside is not only a thing of beauty, but also serves for utilitarian purposes as well. Now, now,…don't think that I cannot hear the low murmur of your voices, conning over your lessons like the hum of a bees hive. I can. And I shall be apt to interrupt your rumbling with the voice of your master. A sound you may interpret as authoritative, commanding, menacing. But let me give assurance, nothing will speak so plainly as the voice of this little twig of birch as I urge you, tardy loiterer, along the flowery path of knowledge. You'll learn that I am conscientious and ever bear in mind the golden maxim. "Spare the rod and you spoil the child". You, my little scholars, will certainly not be spoiled. Don't think, however, that I enjoy the doling out of punishment upon your hands and backsides. I am not one of those cruel potentates who joy in the smart of their subjects. On the contrary, you'll find I administer justice with discrimination rather than severity. The innocent foil to a guilty party's shenanigans will be passed by with indulgence, yet the claims of justice will be satisfied by inflicting a double portion on some little, tough, wrong-headed, broad-skirted, Dutch urchin. *(At this he places the Dunce cap on some unsuspecting member of the audience.)* Oh, you can sulk and swell and grow dogged and sullen beneath the birch. But all this is simply doing my duty by your parents. And I will never inflict a chastisement without following it by the assurance that you will remember it and thank me for it the longest day you have to live. *(He pulls out a pocket watch and checks the minutes of the hour so as not to release the pupils a second early.)* Class…is…now…dismissed!

*(He rings his hand-bell to signal the closing of
school hours. Knickerbocker enters.)*

Scene 6. *"From the Vedders to the Van Rippers"*

KNICKERBOCKER

Up until now, Ichabod Crane had taken up residence at the Inn of Nicholaus Vedder, a patriarch of the village and landlord of "The Vedder Inn", a fine country boardinghouse whose weekly rate became more of a burden than the pedagogue could carry.

(Enter Ichabod followed by Nicholaus and Mrs. Vedder. They come from the direction of the Vedder's Inn.)

MRS. VEDDER

We're so sorry you have to leave us, Mynheer Crane.

ICHABOD

The revenue arising from my school is small and has been scarcely sufficient to furnish me with room and board. Therefore I'm afraid I can no longer afford your fine accommodations.

MRS. VEDDER

This comes as most unwelcome news. You were such a tidy boarder. Perhaps if we were to lower your weekly contributions. Couldn't we do that, Dear?

(Nicholaus Vedder says nothing, but continues his unsettling stare of disapproval at Crane. Ichabod senses the tension and jumps in.)

ICHABOD

No, Mrs. Vedder. I'm afraid I can't ask you to do that. You have already given me a most reasonable rate and I shall take advantage of your good graces no longer. No, I shall have to refuse your kind offer.

MRS. VEDDER

But where will you go, Myneer Crane? We simply can't throw you out onto the streets like a common vagrant. Can we, Dear?

(Again, Nicholaus says nothing, but imagines the possibilities as he puts his pipe into his mouth.)

ICHABOD

I am a man, Mrs. Vedder.

MRS. VEDDER

(considering his statement)

Yes, well, nonetheless,…perhaps we can assist you in finding affordable lodging.

(In music, the three make their way to the mortuary of Mort Vanderghast, Undertaker of Sleepy Hollow.)

CRAYON

The Vedders, being compassionate to his plight, promptly dispatched him to the one place they knew Ichabod could find a nice, satin pillow, stretch-out his legs, and not be disturbed by his fellow boarders. They introduced him to Mort Vanderghast, Undertaker of Sleepy Hollow.

(When they arrive, Mrs. Vedder pulls a string at the back of Vanderghast's business which rings a bell. Vanderghast steps out, having just been working. He wears a long, white apron which is absolutely caked with the blood and fluid of his "clients". There can be no doubt whatever, about the nature of his profession.)

CRAYON

There is a solemn respect paid by the traveler when passing the undertaker's sign in these sequestered places. The stroke of death makes a wider space in the village circle, and is an awful event in the tranquil uniformity of rural life. Mort Vanderghast had been the town's master of funerals for many years.

(Vanderghast greets the visitors. They do not take Vanderghast's hand but all nod politely. The Vedders gesture to Crane as if making the necessary introductions. They wave goodbye and leave the scene, heading back to the Vedder Inn. The two men are in the middle of conversation when the music and narration ends.)

VANDERGHAST

I see,...

ICHABOD

...the arrangement would be temporary, Myneer Vanderghast. As I am just beginning my office as Schoolmaster, I shall find independent lodging upon my first weekly compensation.

VANDERGHAST

You can stay as long as you like. Just remember, this is no hotel. No bed linen here, only shrouds.

ICHABOD

Shrouds?

VANDERGHAST

No fresh-cut roses to smell, only formaldehyde.

ICHABOD

Formaldehyde?

VANDERGHAST

And I've no dining quarters here. You'll have your morning repast in the casket parlor.

ICHABOD

Casket Parlor?

VANDERGHAST

It's all I've got. You can use a display coffin for your breakfast table. Just close the box firmly, sit down and eat. When you're done, be on your way, but wipe the lid down with a damp cloth as we hold visitations in the afternoon.

ICHABOD

I'm not sure...

VANDERGHAST

And one other thing, if you arrive long after dark, the lamps may have been snuffed out. Be careful where you bed-down. Wouldn't want you to wind up on the wrong table, now would we?

ICHABOD

Wr-Wr-Wr-Wrong table?

(The bell rings, signifying another client. Ichabod is startled)

VANDERGHAST

Nothing to worry about, Master Crane. I'll give you a tour of the place when I return.

ICHABOD

I think I'll just be...

VANDERGHAST

I go and it is done: the bell invites me.
Fear it not, Myneer; for it is a knell
That summons us to heaven or to hell.

(The bell rings more loudly this time)

VANDERGHAST

I only hope it's someone trying to get in, and not trying to get out. If you follow my meaning. Please excuse me, Master Crane.

(He exits into his lobby. Crane, clearly shaken by the prospects of rooming in Vanderghast's mortuary, begins to have second thoughts. Throughout the following, Crane peers in through Vanderghast's windows, snoops around the front, picking up a grave-digger's shovel, he then puts it aside in fear, he then peeks inside an unfinished empty coffin which Vanderghast had been building. He finds a simple wooden cross for a pauper's grave. Lifts it, holds it in front of him as if practicing to ward off evil spirits, then puts it back on the ground.)

CRAYON

A curious profession, that of the undertaker. The intention seems to be to soften the horrors of the tomb, to beguile the mind from brooding over the disgraces of perishing mortality. There is a dismal process going on in the grave, ere dust can return to its kindred dust, which the imagination shrinks from contemplating! The trappings of Vanderghast's mystery surrounded Ichabod Crane. Phantom thoughts of demonic persuasion invaded his mind. He envisioned the dead wakening from the deep thick of sleep only to enter his chamber and snuff him out as one of Vanderghast's oil lamps. Crane had made his decision. He would not spend the first night there, lest the territorial spirits of previous "boarders" consider him an un-invited guest.

(Vanderghast re-enters from his lobby. Crane is bent over just at the moment that Vanderghast opens his door wide enough to bump Crane's head, causing him to fall backward into the coffin. This action causes the lid to slam shut.

15

Crane screams as Vanderghast bursts into laughter and lifts open the lid to help the poor man out.)

VANDERGHAST

Oh, my dear Master Crane! Get out of there! It's a bit early for that, if you follow my meaning!

(Vanderghast now has helped Crane completely out of the coffin.)

ICHABOD

Thank you, Myneer Vanderghast,...

(Vanderghast helps brush sawdust off of Crane's shoulders)

ICHABOD

Need you attend to your business?

VANDERGHAST

False alarm. Turns out old man Bummel wasn't dead at all. Only intoxicated. Now, how about that tour?

ICHABOD

I sincerely, thank you, Myneer Vanderghast. Your hospitality is most humbling. However, I have reconsidered and cannot accept. You see, the Reverend Cotton Mather, of whom I am a loyal disciple, is a most notable and honorable authority in the dynamics of the hereafter. I'm afraid he would not approve. A living soul abed in a mortuary would create a most potent alchemy for the devil's playground. And witches and devils have no place in a house of the dead.

VANDERGHAST

You've nothing to worry about here, Myneer. My business is one of sanctity.

ICHABOD

All the same, if you could be so kind as to suggest an alternative dwelling?

VANDERGHAST

Very well. I could refer you to the Van Rippers. They are simple ranchers who may have a spare loft. I'll take you to them. It's too bad, really. I think you might enjoy learning about the processes of death... *(suddenly becoming morose)* I've watched men die, you know. It's a beautiful thing in its own way. The bed of death, with all it stifled griefs - The last testimonies of expiring love! *(He grabs Crane's hand, as though he himself is in the throws of expiration)* The feeble, fluttering, thrilling - oh! how thrilling! - pressure of the hand! The faint, faltering accents, struggling in breath to give one more assurance of affection! The last fond look of the glazing eye, turned upon us even from the threshold of existence! ...*(Pause, appears to come back into "this" world)* You sure you won't reconsider?

ICHABOD

I don't think so.

KNICKER BOCKER

To help out his maintenance, he was, according to country custom in these parts, boarded and lodged at the houses of the farmers, whose children he instructed. With these he lived successively a week at a time, thus going the rounds of the neighborhood, with all his worldly effects tied up in a cotton handkerchief. Vanderghast, being compassionate to his plight, promptly dispatched him to the house of Hans Van Ripper.

(Van Rippers appear from their house.)

MRS. VAN RIPPER

We are happy to take you in, Mynheer Crane.

ICHABOD

Your Christina is an apt pupil and I'm sure that my presence in your home shall make an honorable impression on the child.

<u>VAN RIPPER</u>

Yes, about your accommodations. You wont exactly be living in the house, per se.

<u>ICHABOD</u>

Oh?

<u>MRS. VAN RIPPER</u>

Do you like farm animals, Mynheer Crane?

<u>ICHABOD</u>

Well, I prefer my cattle medium rare on a steaming plate with a sprig of parsley for garnish if that's what you mean?

<u>VAN RIPPER</u>

No, that's not what we mean.

<u>MRS. VAN RIPPER</u>

Your room is,…

<u>VAN RIPPER</u>

Let's call it a "rustic" quarters.

<u>MRS. VAN RIPPER</u>

It's a damp stable. But we have a dry bed of hay.

<u>VAN RIPPER</u>

It's well-ventilated.

<u>MRS. VAN RIPPER</u>

Cracks in the walls and loft. But, we'll give you blankets.

VAN RIPPER

Now, Dear, you make it out to be a pauper's shanty. It isn't as though we haven't kept boarders before.

MRS. VAN RIPPER

That's true. We have. Four horses, three geese, a few hogs, goats, chickens, and mice.

VAN RIPPER

So you'll have a little company!

ICHABOD

I can't thank you enough, Mynheer Van Ripper, Mrs. Van Ripper.

MRS. VAN RIPPER

Well! Would you like to unpack your effects, Mynheer?

ICHABOD

Fine.

MRS. VAN RIPPER

Are you hungry?

ICHABOD

No, no thank you. I'm not hungry. A small thimble of water will be sufficient…well, alright a crust of bread, but I don't want to put you out! Perhaps though, a chop or two of mutton, and maybe brussel sprouts on the side with a dollop of fresh cream or butter on top. A potato couldn't hurt, and then perhaps a flagon of rennish to wash it all down.

VAN RIPPER

I'm just glad he isn't hungry.

ICHABOD

ICHABOD

It has been said of me that though I am lank, I am a healthy feeder and possess the dilating powers of an anaconda.

VAN RIPPER

Welcome home, Ichabod Crane.

(Crane looks in the barn. Sound of a cow mooing. Crane tosses his belongings in.)

ICHABOD

It will do nicely. How shall I ever repay you?

MRS. VAN RIPPER

Well, since you asked. That your teaching services might not be too onerous on the purses of your patrons, who are apt to consider the costs of schooling a grievous burden, and you a mere drone…

VAN RIPPER

There are various ways by which you may render yourself both useful and agreeable.

(Van Ripper tosses a harness in his arms.)

VAN TASSEL

Make the hay,

VEDDER

Mend the fences,

VAN RIPPER

Take the horses to water,

BROUWER

Drive the cows from pasture,

VAN HOUTEN

Cut wood for the winter fire!

(Mrs. Van Ripper sits Ichabod down on a chair, with her daughter Kristina on one knee and a book, another child close by is fed with a wooden spoon and the cradle is rocked by his foot.)

MRS. VAN RIPPER

You'll sit reading with a child on one knee, feed the other, and rock a cradle with your foot. We're off to market!

(She exits with the other ladies. Knickerbocker enters wearing a choir robe. Parson Brouwer and the remaining members of the cast appear as townspeople in matching robes and take their positions around Crane for singing.)

Scene 7. "A Singing Master"

CRAYON

In addition to his other vocations, he was the singing master of the neighborhood. When school hours were over, he would indulge in this, his seemingly more lucrative enterprise. Ichabod Crane would pick up many bright shillings by instructing the young folks in psalmody. On Sundays he would take his station in front of the church gallery, with a band of chosen singers; where, in his own mind, he completely carried away the palm from the parson.

(Knickerbocker joins the rest of the choir as Parson Brouwer raises a baton. There is an excited hustle and bustle and general hubbub among the choir. Brouwer has to quiet them down.)

BROUWER

Brothers,....Now, Sisters! Attention, please! Thank you. Sing nice and full this Sabbath and delight the congregation in the fruits of our labor. Now, let's all come together and lift our voices to the Lord. Ready? Voices up!

(He taps his baton and leads the small group in a musical psalm. It is Kremser, from Nederlandtsch Gedenckclank, 1626. ["We gather together to ask the Lord's blessing"] accapella, well sung, simple and with nice harmony. It should be hauntingly beautiful. Ichabod's voice appropriately rises above the others. It is, however, too nasal to be ignored. The song comes to a close.)

BROUWER

That will do for now. If you'll bow your heads, we'll ask the good
Lord to bless us.

(All bow their heads.)

Dear Heavenly Father, we ask your blessing upon our humble voices this morning. Let us make a joyful noise unto you. Be us ever mindful of Isaiah, Chapter 35, 6th verse, when you said "The tongue of the dumb shall sing!" Amen. The parishioners should be arriving soon. I shall meet you all in the sanctuary. Remember, voices up! Voices up!

(Parson Brouwer dismisses everyone and heads to the church doors. Ichabod Crane crosses to downstage right and begins to gather his books and personal effects, as the choir group breaks apart and gradually make their way into the church. Katrina stays behind to join Ichabod.)

KATRINA

Have you read all these books, Myneer Crane?

ICHABOD

Yes, I have read several volumes quite through *(He shows her his favorite book)* and I am a perfect master of Cotton Mather's "History of Witchcraft, A New England Almanac", in which, by the way, I most firmly and potently believe.

(She takes the book from him and thumbs through its pages.)

KATRINA

Witchcraft? Do you practice as well?

ICHABOD

Good heavens, no! It's only a fascination. Around here a person can get put to death from mere suspicion of witchery.

KATRINA

I wouldn't worry. We haven't pressed anyone to death in almost a hundred years.

ICHABOD

True enough.

(She finds a chapter title in the book that interests her. She reads aloud.)

KATRINA

"Spells of Love and Enchantment"? Is this how you win the hearts of women?

(He gently takes the book from Katrina's hands and closes the cover. He packs it away.)

ICHABOD

I profess not to know how women's hearts are wooed and won. To me they have always been matters of riddle and admiration.

KATRINA

And what am I? A woman to be riddled or admired?

ICHABOD

You, Katrina, are one to be cherished.

KATRINA

That's very sweet, Myneer Crane, but…

ICHABOD

Ichabod, please.

KATRINA

Alright, Ichabod. But what assurance have I that you don't shower such niceties to all your female students of psalmody?

ICHABOD

None, I suppose. But I say nothing without sincerity. I'll never lie to you, Katrina.

KATRINA

Do I have your word?

ICHABOD

You have my word as a gentleman. And that's a sure beginning.

KATRINA

Indeed. Honesty is the way to a woman's heart.

ICHABOD

Good to know. Women's hearts are oft impenetrable. They seem to have but one vulnerable point of access.

KATRINA

Not all. Some have countless avenues, and may be captured in a thousand different ways.

ICHABOD

And you? Does your heart possess so many portals of entry?

KATRINA

Well, the only way to discover the entrance to a castle is to turn the key in every lock. And if that fails, storm the breach like Prince Hal. For a man must battle for his fortress at every door and window. He who does less lacks heart, nobility, courage. He is no man at all. But he who fights for what he wants is a knight in my book. He who reigns supreme over the heart of a woman is indeed a hero…Are you a hero, Ichabod?

ICHABOD

That depends. Are you a battlement to be conquered?

KATRINA

You answered a question with a question. They say people who do that are manipulative. What do you think about that?

ICHABOD

What do you think I think about that?

(They both laugh.)

KATRINA

That's very good. You're clever.

ICHABOD

And you're perceptive.

(The church bells ring. Katrina stands to go in. Judith Gardinier, a purveyor of meats and vegetables enters with a wagon of produce. She observes Ichabod and Katrina discreetly.)

KATRINA

May your cleverness win you the heart of a fair maiden.

ICHABOD

And may your perception find you a hero.

KATRINA

You'll be the first to know.

(Katrina is at the church doors.)

ICHABOD

Do I have your word?

KATRINA

You have my attention, Ichabod. And that's a sure beginning.

(Katrina exits)

JUDITH

A fine catch for some fortunate gentleman.

ICHABOD

Pardon?

JUDITH

The young lady with whom you were speaking. Was it not Juliet's nurse who reasoned, "He that can lay hold of her, shall have the chinks"?

ICHABOD

Indeed it was…The lass comes from a prominent family to be sure.

JUDITH

Indeed. She stands to inherit all that her father doth possess. I should know. I service the Van Tassel cupboard.

(Extends her hand to Crane. He takes it.)

JUDITH

Judith Gardinier, Purveyor of fine meats and vegetable fare.

ICHABOD

Ichabod Crane, Pedagogue.

JUDITH

You are no doubt familiar with the Van Tassel estate?

ICHABOD

Yes, but my heart yearns after the damsel who is to inherit those domains.

JUDITH

Katrina Van Tassel.

ICHABOD

Even she!

JUDITH

And tell me truthfully, Is it your heart which yearns, or your purse?

ICHABOD

Why whatever are you suggesting?

JUDITH

If you hadn't known of her father's wealth when you first encountered the girl, would you still have been so taken by her?

ICHABOD

Miss Gardinier, certain it is, every relationship has its,…shall we say, fringe benefits?

JUDITH

There it is, all for the taking! The plantation of Mynheer Van Tassel! Look upon that sumptuous promise of luxurious winter fare! Picture to yourself every roasting pig running about with a pudding in his belly and an apple in his mouth; the pigeons snugly put to bed in a comfortable pie, and tucked in with a coverlet of crust. The geese are swimming in their own gravy; and the ducks pairing cozily in dishes like snug married couples.

ICHABOD

Snug married couples?! Is that how they are?

JUDITH

Roll your great green eyes over the fat meadow lands, the rich fields of wheat, of rye, of buckwheat, and Indian corn, and orchards…

(Hands him a ripe red apple. He bites.)

burthened with ruddy fruit, which surround the warm tenement of Van Tassel!

ICHABOD

The Van Tassel orchards!

JUDITH

Expand your imagination with the idea how they might be readily turned into cash, and the money invested in immense tracts of wild land, and shingle palaces in the wilderness.

ICHABOD

Nay, my busy fancy is already realizing my hopes!

JUDITH

Imagine, you and the blooming Katrina with a whole family of children, mounted on the top of a wagon loaded with household trumpery, with pots and kettles dangling beneath; and you yourself bestriding a pacing mare, with a colt at her heels, setting out for…

ICHABOD

Kentucky, Tennessee…

JUDITH

Or the Lord knows where!

(Ichabod suddenly snaps out of his fantasies.)

ICHABOD

What's your interest in my prosperity?

JUDITH

I trust you'd remember the little people who helped you along?

ICHABOD

I believe the Latin term is "quid pro quo".

JUDITH

Commerce, Mynheer Crane. Simple commerce.

(Judith grips the handles of her wagon and rolls it off to Exit.)

ICHABOD

But I haven't paid you for the apple, Miss Gardinier!

(Judith turns back to him with a knowing smile.)

JUDITH

You will.

(Judith Gardinier exits.)

ICHABOD

Till we meet again, Miss Gardinier!

(Ichabod pulls out a small book and quill and begins to write.)

ICHABOD

"Sunday, October twenty and seven, in the year of our Lord, 1795. Among the musical disciples who assemble, one morning each week to receive my instructions in psalmody, is Katrina Van Tassel, the daughter and only child of a substantial Dutch farmer, Baltus Van Tassel. She is a blooming lass of fresh eighteen, plump as a partridge, ripe and melting, and rosy-cheeked as one of her father's peaches, and universally famed, not merely for her beauty, but her vast expectations. She is withal a little of a coquette, as might be perceived even in her dress, which is a mixture of ancient and modern fashions, as most suited to set off her charms. In addition, she wears a provokingly short petticoat, to display the prettiest foot and ankle in the country around…I think she fancies me."

Scene 8. "Fireside Tales"

(Ichabod goes directly to the pre-set scene of Mrs. Van Ripper's parlor. Mrs. Van Ripper, Mrs. Van Tassel, Mrs. Vedder, Judith Gardinier and Katrina are cozily spinning yarn for quilts and roasting apples on a fire. Ichabod Crane sits amidst the ladies, and holds court.)

MRS. VEDDER

We are so fortunate to be graced with the presence of such an astute and learned man. You are always welcome to indulge in this, another source of your fearful pleasures; passing long, cold evenings by the fire with us.

MRS. VAN RIPPER

Myneer Crane, you've made quite an impression amongst our circle of ladies!

ICHABOD

Mrs. Van Ripper, I cannot tell you what an auspicious honor it is to be in your home, among you fine ladies as you sit spinning in the parlor, a row of apples roasting and spluttering along the hearth…

MRS. VAN RIPPER

The pleasure is ours, Mynheer Crane.

KATRINA

—storyteller

I told you, he was as entertaining a raconteur as he is a singer.

MRS. VAN TASSEL

We so enjoy your fascinating talks on Galileo, Astronomy, and the laws of gravity!

ICHABOD

Indeed, I have many theories and speculations on comets, shooting stars, and the vast universe which enraptures ordinary man with its mystery.

KATRINA

Why just the other day, Mynheer Crane was telling me that the earth doesn't at all sit still as so many would have us believe, but it actually moves!

MRS. VAN TASSEL

The earth moves?

MRS. VEDDER

Is it possible?

MRS. VAN RIPPER

Do tell us, Myneer Crane!

ICHABOD

Well, to put it plain,…the earth upon which we all reside, is simply one monolithic ball in the hands of God. But gravity, a physiological precept conjured by the creator himself, holds mankind firmly to the globe's crust like a gigantic magnet. After long hours of careful meditation on the subject, I have concluded that the world absolutely turns round and round and that we are half the time topsy-turvy!

ALL

Simply amazing! That's incredible! Alarming! I don't believe it!

ICHABOD

Oh, yes! It's all true, Miladies. But such unexplained phenomenon perhaps is not the most appropriate subject matter for you more refined womenfolk.

ALL

What?! Pshaw! The devil you say! Oh, yes?!

MRS. VAN TASSEL

These environs are as appropriate a place as any for tales of the unnatural.

(Forboding music gently creeps in and lights begin to dim.)

GARDINIER

We can regale you with many strange tales of ghosts and goblins,...

KATRINA

haunted fields,...

MRS. VAN RIPPER

haunted brooks,...

MRS. VEDDER

haunted bridges,...

MRS. VAN TASSEL

haunted houses,...

MRS. VEDDER

And of course the galloping Hessian of the Hollow, or as he is most often referred, "the headless horseman"!

ICHABOD

(visibly unnerved.)

Hea- hea- hea- head-less horseman?

MRS. VAN RIPPER

Now, Mynheer Crane! Surely, you know of the Hessian trooper!

ICHABOD

No, but I have a feeling you're all about to enlighten me.

MRS. VEDDER

It is said that one British soldier decapitated in the war and vengeful because of the act, rises from his crypt, horse and all, and seeks out the soul responsible for his death.

MRS. VAN TASSEL

He has been heard several times of late, patrolling the country.

MRS. VAN RIPPER

He tethers his horse nightly among the graves in the churchyard,

MRS. VEDDER

And wields a sickle or saber to lop off the head of anyone he suspects is the culprit.

KATRINA

Parson Brouwer himself had an encounter.

GARDINIER

Yes, he met the horseman returning from his foray into Sleepy Hollow and was obliged to get up behind him. On they galloped over bush and brake, over hill and swamp until they reached the old bridge when the horseman suddenly threw old Brouwer into the brook, and hurled his own severed head in the direction of the Parson. The Hessian vanished. And Parson Brouwer, by the grace of God, lived to tell the tale.

33

MRS. VEDDER

Old Brouwer has oft described the demon spirit. He is dark, dressed in black. The fleshy folds of skin where once his head joined his body have begun to rot. But the wound itself still appears fresh. The muscle fiber from the throat is exposed. Gurgling sounds can be heard through his windpipe as blood flows freely from the open hole at the base of his neck.

(Music out. Lights restore.)

MRS. VAN RIPPER

More cranberry sauce, Mynheer Crane?

ICHABOD

No, Mrs. Van Ripper. I believe I've had all I can stomach. I cannot say that your tales are not distressing. All these, however, are mere terrors of the night, phantoms of the mind that walk in darkness. I have seen many spectres in my time, and been more than once beset by Satan in diverse shapes, in my lonely perambulations, but daylight puts an end to all these evils, and I am then able to pass a pleasant life of it in spite of the devil and all his works…that is, given the morning sun will yet rise another day. Well, speaking of which, it is rather late.

(Ladies rise.)

MRS. VEDDER

Leaving so soon?

ICHABOD

Yes, I must be going now.

MRS. VAN TASSEL

Oh. And we so wanted to hear more about your methods in pedagogy. There's so much still that we have yet to know about you.

GARDINIER

The most important thing about Mynheer Crane is that he is worthy husband material.

(The ladies love the comment and all react accordingly. Ichabod feins embarrassment.)

ICHABOD

Now, Judith!

GARDINIER

I'm acquainted with him well enough. I'll tell you all that I know over more coffee.

MRS. VAN TASSEL

Shall we to the kitchen, then?

GARDINIER

Come Katrina, I think you'll find what I have to say equally of interest.

KATRINA

Alright.

MRS. VAN TASSEL

Very well. Goodnight, Mynheer Crane.

KATRINA

Goodnight, Ichabod.

(The three exit into the Van Ripper "kitchen")

ICHABOD

By the way,…at just what hour is sunrise?

35

(Mrs. Van Ripper senses his apprehension and makes an attempt to calm him.)

MRS. VAN RIPPER

Mynheer Crane, the barn is only down the old dirt road apiece. You'll be safe in your bunk and fast asleep before you know it.

ICHABOD

Yes, I'm sure you're right. Good evening, Ladies.

MRS. VEDDER

Pleasant dreams.

(Mrs. Vedder and Mrs. Van Ripper exit. Ichabod Crane dons his hat and ventures out into the night. Forboding music and sounds of the dark woods surround him. He startles and quakes with each new and horrifying sound.)

ICHABOD

Whatever comfort the Van Ripper's crackling wood fire gives, where no spectre dares show his face,...It is dearly purchased by the terrors of my subsequent walks homeward, however brief to their barn. What fearful shapes and shadows beset my path amidst the dim and ghastly glare of a chill-filled night! How I am thrown into complete dismay at the idea that every rushing blast or howling among the trees may be this galloping Hessian on one of his midnight scourings!

(Finally, he makes a run.)

Scene 9. "Levitation"

(Ichabod arrives at the schoolhouse, opens the door and steps inside. He lights a lantern and is shocked by what he sees. Schoolhouse objects and furniture virtually appear to be in a slow state of levitation as they lift off the floor

and make their way to the ceiling. Musical cue such as a simple bow drawn across the strings of a violin accompanies the rising.)

ICHABOD

Angels and ministers of grace defend us! What manner of black magician can render chairs, desks, inkwells, lamps and quills unto this state of ascension? What creeping creatures have crept into my schoolhouse at night, in spite of Heer Van Houten's formidable fastenings of withe and window stakes? It is certain! All the witches in the country must hold their clandestine gatherings here. Oh horror of horrors!

(The objects should now be their highest possible point in the schoolhouse. Suddenly, from behind the schoolhouse unit, Brom Bones, Derrick Van Bummel, and Jonathan Doolittle appear. They are all holding on to the ends of ropes and it is clear they are the ones who created the illusion designed to scare Ichabod out of his wits. They explode into laughter. Ichabod, nonplussed, sees the rope and puts it all together. The boys lower the objects.)

ICHABOD

Ruffians!

BONES

Boo!

(Startled, Ichabod screams and falls backward. Bones and his Sleepy Hollow boys begin making ghostly moans and caterwalls. They get up into Ichabod's face and then run off into the woods laughing hysterically all the way. Ichabod, stands up and brushes himself off.)

ICHABOD

Morning cannot come quickly enough!

(He takes off in the direction of the barn.)

CRAYON

Brom Bones drew upon the funds of rustic waggery in his disposition and played off boorish practical jokes upon his rival. Ichabod had become the object of whimsical persecution to Bones and his gang of rough riders. And in this way matters went on for sometime.

(Crayon Exits.)

Scene 10. *"The Gift"*

(Ichabod enters arm in arm with Katrina)

ICHABOD

…but I suppose my favorite epitaph of all is that of William Shakespeare himself:

(As Ichabod begins reciting the following epitaph, we see Brom Bones hiding behind a tree to spy on the two.)

"Good friend, for Jesus' sake forbeare
To dig the dust enclosed here.
Blessed be he that spares these stones,
And curst be he that moves my bones."

KATRINA

Why that's really very…macabre, Ichabod.

ICHABOD

I thought you'd like it. I have something for you.

(He hands her the almanac on the history of witchcraft.)

KATRINA

This is your copy of Cotton Mather's "History of Witchcraft, A New England Almanac".

ICHABOD

It's yours now. Keep it as long as I have your heart.

KATRINA

Thank you, Ichabod. I shall.

(They Exit)

Scene 11. *"The Exhibition"*

CRAYON

The next day, Brom Bones offered a show of physical prowess for all to see. It was clear that his secretive discussion with Baltus Van Tassel on Sunday morning and Ichabod's apparent courtship of Katrina led to the exhibition designed to steal Katrina's heart.

(Brom Bones enters with Van Bummel and Doolittle. Bones' minions help to announce the exhibition with horns and banners)

BROM BONES

Good people of Sleepy Hollow, Tarry Town! And all parts from Greensburgh to the Tappan Zee! Let the exhibition begin! For Behold! I have arrived! *(At this point the crowd has assembled around him.)* Before this day is done, I'll prove myself the only worthy suitor for the heart of one Katrina Van Tassel! For I, Abraham Van Brunt am hero of the country road. My feats of strength and hardihood are known throughout this hollow, Tarry Town and beyond! Let the examination begin!

MRS. VAN RIPPER

Why should you win the young Van Tassel's affection?

BROM BONES

Because I'm handsome.

MRS. VAN TASSEL

Can you carry firewood?

BROM BONES

For that, I'm broad-shouldered.

KATRINA

Can you write with both hands?

BROM BONES

Yes, I'm double-jointed.

MRS. VAN RIPPER

Are you strong?

BROM BONES

My frame is that of Hercules!

VAN HOUTEN

Have you a brain?

BROM BONES

I am famed for great knowledge in horsemanship.

VAN RIPPER

But can you ride?

BROM BONES

I'm as dexterous on horseback as a Tartar, but you toy with me, you all ask questions for which you know the answers. I know what you think of me. You know what I think of myself. I want to know what Katrina thinks of me.

KATRINA

I think no more of you than I think of Ichabod.

BROM BONES

You'll agree I possess a bluff but not altogether unpleasant countenance?

KATRINA

Perhaps, but a man is only as fair as is proved by his actions.

BROM BONES

I'm very active! I'll attend any scene of feud or merriment for miles around. I am foremost at all races and cockfights; I am always ready for either a fight or a frolic. When any madcap prank or rustic brawl occurs in the vicinity you can warrant Brom Bones is at the bottom of it! In short, I'm arrogant, but fun.... Enough talk! Let the challenge begin! Will it be tomahawk throwing? Arm wrestling? Wood chopping? I am in form and spirit, a supple jack - I am pliable, yet firm. Yielding, but tough. Though I bend, I never break. At the slightest pressure, I roll, I jab, I swing, I sway, I make minced meat of my prey. Once victorious, I am erect and carry my head as high as ever! Now, be there any man alive who can best me? Shall it be the schoolmaster who'll accept my challenge? Let Ichabod Crane come forth and I will break open his pate like a gourd, I'll whip his innards into a Christmas pudding, I'll sling him about like an infant's plaything!

KATRINA

Why Mynheer Crane, Brom Bones? He's not so much as spoken a harsh word against you.

BROM BONES

He's my rival for your affections is he not? I've seen the way he eyes your tender, yet desire-provoking ankles, I've spied how he vies for your affections and I've marked his poetic though pathetic attempts at courtship. Will you deny it?

KATRINA

No, I cannot deny it.

BROM BONES

Come then, the gauntlet is tossed.

KATRINA

On behalf of Mynheer Crane, I respectfully decline. He is too conscious of the superior might of his adversary to enter the lists against him. You have the obvious advantage as your might displays. He therefore could not win such a match. Ichabod's prowess lies not in his physical strength but in his mind, heart and soul.

BROM BONES

Will he concede defeat, then?

KATRINA

No. He will not fight you, nor will he concede defeat. He shall win my love upon his own terms, not yours. And if she will accept my declarations, I will prove the better suitor. For we will soon see who can best speak the language of love. That is my challenge for you. Now, if you will all excuse me, I have a voice lesson.

(Katrina exits)

Scene 12. "A Challenge"

VAN BRUNT

You see this, Derrick? Just as I suspected. No one man enough even to arm wrestle.

(The crowd, still as statues, simply stares silently at Van Brunt. He becomes angry.)

VAN BRUNT

Well what are you all staring at? You may as well go about your business! Is it not enough a man must be humbled by the girl he loves but he must be humiliated publicly as well? Go on! There's no show here!

42

(The crowd dissembles and gradually the townsfolk make their way back to their homes, trades, etc. Brom Bones is left with Van Bummel. Just as Peter Vanderdonk is leaving, Brom Bones stops him.)

VAN BRUNT

You! Vanderdonk!

(Vanderdonk stops, turns round to face Brom Bones.)

VANDERDONK

I am Peter Vanderdonk.

VAN BRUNT

Will you deliver a message to the schoolmaster?

VANDERDONK

A message, sir? I trust it is worth a schilling.

(Brom Bones pays him.)

VAN BRUNT

At least. Tell Ichabod Crane that if he wants the exclusive attentions of Katrina Van Tassel, he shall have to best me first.

VANDERDONK

Miss Van Tassel has already indicated that he is a gentleman and will not fight you.

VAN BRUNK

Alright. Fair enough. This Crane fancies himself a cavalier? Let us then compete using the weapons of true gentlemen...swords. Let's call it, "Best in the art of swordplay". "Last Man Standing." Van Bummel shall be my sparring partner and second. I suggest Crane take up lessons immediately. Let the duel commence at three of the clock this afternoon. Here.

VANDERDONK

Swords, sir?

VAN BUMMEL

That's what he said. Maybe you don't know what a sword is.

VANDERDONK

On the contrary, I was born with one in my right hand. And I shall be glad to deliver this message to Mynheer Crane. For I will offer my services as his partner in sparring and his second at the duel. Now, while your company is most engaging, I must leave you if Mynheer Crane is to prepare for your whipping at 3 of the clock.

(He turns to leave.)

VAN BUMMEL

You're an errand boy!

(The comment stops Vanderdonk in his tracks. He turns to Van Bummel.)

VANDERDONK

Yes, but I'm an errand boy with a rapier. Any time you want a message from me, I'll be sure to "deliver". Gentlemen.

(Vanderdonk exits. Van Bummel makes a move as if to lunge for Vanderdonk. Brom Bones stops him.)

VAN BRUNT

Pay him no mind. This is between Crane and myself. Let Vanderdonk school him in the art all he desires. He has only till the strike of three. I shall double the schoolmaster up and lay him on a shelf of his own schoolhouse.

CRAYON

Such was the formidable rival with whom Ichabod Crane had to

44

contend, and considering all things, stouter men than him would have shrunk from the competition. However, from the moment Ichabod made his interests known, a deadly feud gradually arose between him and the burly warrior of Sleepy Hollow.

Scene 13. *"Swords are Crossed"*

(Music. Brom Bones and Derrick Van Bummel, his sparring partner, enter with fencing gear in a "courtyard". Ichabod Crane and Peter Vanderdonk, his sparring partner enter with cruder gear in a "stable". The sparring ensues on both sides and Bones exhibits the swordsman skills of a master while Crane barely knows which end of his weapon is to be held. While the four men are sparring in two separate locations, a townsperson enters each scene and alerts each pair as the other's sparring. The four men gradually spar their way to the center of the town square, encounter the others and Bones attacks Crane. The townspeople of the Hollow gradually congregate to witness the fight. Cheers and jeers from the crowd. They fight until the scene climaxes in Bones gaining the upper hand as Crane is disarmed, prostrate, exhausted and Bones positions a foot amidst Crane's chest in the traditional pose befitting a hunter with his kill. The crowd gives a final cheer, music reaches its climax, crowd freezes, lights out.)

END OF ACT ONE

ACT II

Scene 1. *"The Van Tassels at Home"*

(Mr. and Mrs. Van Tassel on their piazza. They are busy with preparations for their annual quilting frolic. They are also in the midst of argument.)

MRS. VAN TASSEL

It's disgraceful!

VAN TASSEL

Brom Bones won the duel fair and square.

MRS. VAN TASSEL

Be that as it may, it turned into a public spectacle much to the shame of Master Crane.

VAN TASSEL

He accepted the duel!

MRS. VAN TASSEL

Brom Bones didn't need to embarrass the poor man.

VAN TASSEL

My Love, a little embarrassment is the least of hazards endemic in a duel of swords. He could very well have killed the schoolmaster, afterall.

MRS. VAN TASSEL

That's very nice. We've come to battle of physical superiority over wits.

VAN TASSEL

He accepted the duel!

MRS. VAN TASSEL

And you encouraged Brom Bones to compete for Katrina's interest!

VAN TASSEL

I encouraged an exhibition of strength…

MRS. VAN TASSEL

You admit it!

VAN TASSEL

I said nothing to him about a duel!

MRS. VAN TASSEL

You didn't have to. Young men are quick to interpret an elder's words for their own purposes.

VAN TASSEL

Abraham's a good boy. He only means to impress Katrina.

MRS. VAN TASSEL

At the risk of possible injury to our Hollow's schoolmaster.

VAN TASSEL

It's over now.

MRS. VAN TASSEL

You'd do well to let Katrina's affections run their course, wherever they may.

VAN TASSEL

It is true, I seldom send either my eyes or my thoughts beyond the boundaries of my daughter and farm.

MRS. VAN TASSEL

Yes, but within those boundaries everything is snug, happy, and well-conditioned. We are prosperous enough and will remain so without worrying over who our daughter will one day choose to marry.

VAN TASSEL

I am satisfied with my wealth, but not proud of it. There is a difference. While I do pique myself upon a hearty abundance, I make no gaudy show in the style that I live.

MRS. VAN TASSEL

I'm not denying that. I am simply saying Crane is a more suitable for Katrina than the blacksmith.

VAN TASSEL

Listen, I'm an easy indulgent soul. I love Katrina better even than my pipe, and, like a reasonable man and an excellent father, I let her have her way in everything. But, like most fathers I am suspicious of the motives of every soul who comes to court my daughter.

MRS. VAN TASSEL

Doesn't the farm keep you occupied? I have enough to do to attend to my housekeeping and manage my poultry. Therefore I've learned ducks and geese are foolish things and must be looked after, but girls can take care of themselves.

VAN TASSEL

Can they?

MRS. VAN TASSEL

They can without the meddlesome interference of parents.

VAN TASSEL

What's this Crane after, anyway?

MRS. VAN TASSEL

He has a soft and foolish heart toward the girl. Why should we wonder that so tempting a morsel finds favor in his eyes?

VAN TASSEL

Tempting a morsel? She's our daughter, not a strudel!

MRS. VAN TASSEL

Of course, Dear. And Ichabod Crane is a red-blooded man no less subject to the allures of youthful beauty than is the blacksmith Van Brunt.

VAN TASSEL

He makes his advances to her in a quiet and gently insinuating manner. His visits to our farm are more and more frequent.

MRS. VAN TASSEL

Voice lessons! He is, afterall, her singing master.

VAN TASSEL

It's a perfect ruse....Entering such a prosperous family would be quite a promotion for a schoolteacher, would it not?

MRS. VAN TASSEL

Baltus Van Tassel, I'm ashamed you would even suggest that Master Crane has ulterior motives.

VAN TASSEL

It happens, Dear. A stranger moves into town. Professes his love for a well-to-do young lass. She gives her heart away, they marry, and before you know it, the fellow has moved in, inherited her father's wealth and taken off for Amsterdam!... I just don't want to be taken. More importantly, I don't want her to get taken...

(Katrina enters and overhears the next question.)

VAN TASSEL

How old is this man, anyway?

KATRINA

Old enough to recognize suspecting parents a mile off.

MRS. VAN TASSEL

Your father has concerns over Master Crane's courtings of you.

KATRINA

You needn't worry Vedder. Ichabod Crane is a man of vastly superior taste and accomplishments. Inferior in learning only to the Parson. Mother, I want to invite Myneer Crane to our festivity this evening. He deserves to join our frolic as much as Brom.

VAN TASSEL

Invite him to the...!

MRS. VAN TASSEL

Let Katrina invite him to the merrymaking. It won't hurt to have Master Crane to our feast. Then you yourself can examine the gentleman more closely. You may find more in him than you realize.

VAN TASSEL

(Considering, as he chews his pipe.)

He'll eat everything in sight, you know.

MRS. VAN TASSEL

There's plenty enough food for everyone.

VAN TASSEL

Does he have to sing? Tell me, he won't sing.

KATRINA

He won't sing. He may dance, but he won't sing.

VAN TASSEL

Well, all right. Master Crane is welcome to our autumn feast.

(Katrina wraps her arms around him and kisses his cheek. Mrs. Van Tassel lovingly rubs his back.)

KATRINA

Thank you, Vedder!

(She exits.)

MRS. VAN TASSEL

Thank you.

VAN TASSEL

You're welcome.

(They exit hand-in-hand into the home. As they are exiting, Van Tassel adds...)

He's going to eat everything.

Scene 2. "An Invitation"

(Ichabod is back in the schoolhouse. He addresses the audience.)

ICHABOD

Now, pupils! You see in my hand a familiar object, no doubt. Whether you believe it to be the scepter of despotic power or a birch of justice, I'll hang it here aside the "throne" as a constant terror to evildoers. *(He hangs the switch on a hook on the lectern then holds up a wooden cigar box.)* Now, here I have your various and sundry contraband articles and prohibited weapons, confiscated from the bony little fingers of you idle urchins such as half-munched apples, popguns, whirligigs, fly cages, and whole legions of rampant little paper gamecocks. As for the most recent transgression for which you were all complicit,…and don't pretend you don't recall… When last you were dismissed, books were flung aside without being put away on the shelves, ink-stands were overturned, benches thrown down, and you burst out of the schoolhouse like a legion of young imps, yelping and racketing about the green, in joy at your emancipation. I assure you, today I'll not suffer the bustle and hubbub in this schoolroom. You will, like good scholars, pore over your lessons, without stopping at trifles; those who are nimble will skip over half with impunity, and those who are tardy will have a smart application on the rear to quicken their speed or help them over a tall word. That being said, you will procure your chalk slates, and open your English Literature books to Chaucer's *The Canterbury Tales.*

(Peter Vanderdonk comes running into the classroom out of breath.)

VANDERDONK

Greetings, Mynheer Crane!

ICHABOD

Why Peter! You are full of importance and hurry! What mission is so urgent that you would grace me with your presence this afternoon?

VANDERDONK

You're giving lessons, so I shan't be long. I am to deliver this.

(He hands Crane a folded parchment sealed with the wax imprint of the Van Tassel family crest.)

ICHABOD

Whatever could this be?

(He opens it and reads.)

VANDERDONK

It's an invitation for you to attend a merry-making to be held this evening at the Van Tassel home. I am sent at the bequest of Mynheer Baltus Van Tassel and wife.

ICHABOD

And the occasion?

VANDERDONK

A quilting frolic.

ICHABOD

This evening?! This is rather late notice.

VANDERDONK

Oh yes. I suspect the idea was inspired only this morning. Even now all is bustle and hubbub in the estate for the preparations. It is to be a masked gathering.

ICHABOD

Masked! Oh my!

VANDERDONK

The festivities are to commence at eight of the clock.

ICHABOD

Am I to assume Brom Bones is also invited?

VANDERDONK

He is. Mynheer Van Tassel encourages the two of you to make merry in a neutral setting. In addition, he was heard to say that tapping a cask of wine may do us all some good.

ICHABOD

Indeed it may, indeed it may. And am I to escort the young Van Tassel this evening?

VANDERDONK

The damsel will be in attendance.

ICHABOD

Think you she intends to clutch *my* arm?

VANDERDONK

She will be in attendance, Mynheer.

ICHABOD

But, did she ask for me in particular?

VANDERDONK

The invitation was sent from the Van Tassel household. Katrina Van Tassel certainly resides there. You may conclude it is from the young Katrina herself.

ICHABOD

Ah! Thank you, Peter! But,…She made no specific mention of Brom Bones nor my name to you?

VANDERDONK

While she did not send for you personally, you were not excluded. Though she has not refused the advances of Brom Bones, neither has she accepted his attempts. Now, the lass did not specifically mention your name. But that is not to say that you name did not cross the lips of the damsel. For I happen to know that her current schoolbook of natural wonders is turned to the chapter "Orinthology" and any decent essay on birds must include the "crane", that wading bird off our own New England coasts. And we all know that Katrina reads aloud. We can therefore assume Katrina has uttered the word "Crane" at least once this afternoon.

ICHABOD

Oh, this Katrina, she is clever! Why this is the very craft of young courtship. And it is a game derived to maintain the interests of her suitor. There is now no question but that the girl intends to make her declarations of love for me a public show. This is the very purpose of the merry-making or "quilting frolic". The Van Tassel's fortunes are at hand! The funeral baked meats will coldly furnish forth the marriage tables! A thousand thanks to you, Peter Vanderdonk!

(Crane pays him several bright schillings.)

VANDERDONK

And just as many to you, Mynheer Crane!

(Vanderdonk exits. Crane rings the school bell)

ICHABOD

Class dismissed!!!

(Ichabod strikes his "schoolhouse" and grabs his journal to begin writing)

ICHABOD

"Wednesday, October 30, in the year of our Lord, seventeen hundred and ninety-five. I have just been invited to an affair at the Van Tassel home! The peace of my mind is at an end and my only study now is how to gain the affections of the peerless daughter of Van Tassel! I'll spend an extra half hour at my toilet, and I'll brush up only suit of rusty black. I'll make my appearance before my mistress in the true style of a cavalier. I'll borrow the Van Ripper's horse. I'm bound to make a memorable appearance!

Scene 3. "The Van Ripper's Horse"

(Outside in front of the Van Ripper's stables, Hans Van Ripper and wife are busy putting away tack. Ichabod Crane arrives.)

73

ICHABOD

Afternoon, good landlords!

MRS. VAN RIPPER

You're home early, Mynheer Crane.

ICHABOD

I dismissed my students promptly, as I have to prepare for tonight's festivities at the Van Tassels.

VAN RIPPER

Careful, Crane! You come out here to the stables and I'll put you to work.

MRS. VAN RIPPER

Ignore him. Everyone's entitled to one night off.

VAN RIPPER

Anything we can do for you, Master Crane?

ICHABOD

I'm here to request the use of your finest horse.

VAN RIPPER

My finest horse?

ICHABOD

As I have been invited by Katrina Van Tassel to tonight's merrymaking, I had hoped that I might make an appearance before my mistress in the true style of a cavalier.

VAN RIPPER

Very well, Crane. I'll loan you the finest horse that 'ere trod the Hollow; "Gunpowder"!

ICHABOD

Oh my! With a name like Gunpowder, he's sure to be full of fire and mettle!

MRS. VAN RIPPER

Don't get too excited.

VAN RIPPER

Why it's a fine steed.

MRS. VAN RIPPER

It's a broken down plow horse.

VAN RIPPER

Plow, yes, plow. It's a beast of labor, full of viciousness!

MRS. VAN RIPPER

He's outlived everything else.

VAN RIPPER

Yes, but he's lean and mean!

MRS. VAN RIPPER

He's gaunt and shagged.

VAN RIPPER

His head is unusually shaped....

MRS. VAN RIPPER

Like a hammer.

VAN RIPPER

Now he's just the wee bit unkempt.

MRS. VAN RIPPER

His mane is rusty, his tail is tangled and knotted with burrs.

VAN RIPPER

Yes, but he'll fix you with an eye of spirited fire!

MRS. VAN RIPPER

Yes, he lost the other eye long ago. It hangs a bit out of its socket. Lost its pupil and glares at you all spectral like. A thick, milky film oozes from the...

VAN RIPPER

Alright, alright! Let's not oversell, Dear!

ICHABOD

Mynheer Van Ripper, might I borrow Gunpowder just for the night?

VAN RIPPER

He's all yours!

(They all turn toward the barn. The Van Rippers lead him to the horse.)

Scene 4. "He Designed It!"

(Ichabod Crane and Yost Van Houten enter from opposite sides of the stage and meet in the center)

ICHABOD

Afternoon, Good Mynheer Van Houten!

VAN HOUTEN

Ah, my friend, Mynheer Crane! And to where do your feet take you in such haste?

ICHABOD

I'm on my way to a merry-making to be held at the home of Baltus Van Tassel. Do you know it?

VAN HOUTEN

Know it, my good man? I designed it!

ICHABOD

Did you?

VAN HOUTEN

Indeed. I still have the drawings for that particular farm house, if you'd like to see them.

ICHABOD

Some other time, perhaps. Right now, I must needs traverse to the Van Ripper's barn to borrow a steed.

VAN HOUTEN

I'm on my way to the very same gathering. Never missed a year, I'll give you a hand up onto the horse. You shall need a boost in mounting the beast. Besides, it will give us an opportunity to talk.

ICHABOD

Whatever will we talk about?

VAN HOUTEN

Have you any interest in *architecture*, Mynheer Crane?!

ICHABOD

Well,…

VAN HOUTEN

You see, the Van Tassel home is one of my spacious farmhouses, with high-ridged but lowly sloping roofs, built in the style handed down from the first Dutch settlers. The low projecting eaves form a piazza along the front, which I feel is most...

(They exit as Van Houten enlightens Crane on the topic of architecture more than anyone would care to know.)

KNICKERBOCKER

Yost Van Houten hoisted Ichabod onto the horse. And Ichabod and Gunpowder shambled out of the gate of Hans Ran Ripper like such an apparition as is seldom to be met with in broad daylight. Now, Brom Bones' horse was the very antithesis of Ichabod's kerplopping glue factory. And Brom Bones was proud of his stallion. He was consequently the hero of the scene, having come to the gathering on his favorite steed, "Dare-Devil", a creature like Bones himself, full of mettle and mischief, and which no one but himself could manage. He was, in fact, noted for preferring vicious animals, given to all kinds of tricks, which kept the rider in constant risk of his neck, for he held a tractable well-broken horse as unworthy of a lad of spirit. Upon their arrival, the autumnal festivities were in full swing!

Scene 5. *"An Autumn Feast"*

(Baltus enters the new scene. Lights rise on "The Van Tassel Mansion". This is represented by a couple of festive torchlights and a table center with a smorgasbord of food. Period music plays and the guests have all arrived in costume. The masks worn by the guests denote everything from skeletons and black cats to lions and kings. The guests surround the table with goblets in hand and turn their attention to Baltus Van Tassel.)

BALTUS

Welcome! Welcome! One and all! You are all welcome to the castle Van Tassel for our annual night of revelry and feasting in this sumptuous season! *(The party guests explode in cheers and whistles.)* Let us not, however, stand on ceremony to the exclusion of nourishment, for our appetites, some more than others, must be satiated in the tradition of an authentic Van Tassel spread. And as I stand here this evening, I am aware that all eyes are open to every symptom of culinary abundance, ranged with delight over the treasures of jolly autumn. So without further ado, I present my lovely wife to do the honors. Mrs. Van Tassel, what burgeoning cornucopia have you in store for our taste buds this evening?

MRS. VAN TASSEL

(Teasing them all.) Well, Dear, this year I'm afraid to say I haven't prepared much. *(The crowd responds with laughs and jeers of incredulity.)* Only enough for the king and Queen of Holland! *(crowd cheers)*

BALTUS

I'll make my hospitable attentions brief but sincere, confined to a shake of the hand, a slap on the shoulder, a gentle kiss here and there, in order that you can indulge with reckless abandon as I extend a hearty invitation to fall to and help yourselves!

(They cheer. Throughout the rest of Mrs. Van Tassel's speech, she crosses downstage to "narrate" the menu for the audience as they party guest dig in behind her. The crowd should mime eating in slow motion in order to facilitate the passage of time.)

MRS. VAN TASSEL

Now, just feast your eyes upon these porkers, and a carved-out, sleek side of bacon, and juicy relishing ham, behold every turkey daintily trussed up, with gizzards under wings, and peradventure a necklace of savory sausages; And even bright chanticleer himself lay sprawling on his back, in a side-dish with uplifted claws, as if craving that quarter which his chivalrous spirit disdained to ask while living.

(The crowd reacts favorably.)

MRS. VAN TASSEL

And I'm just beginning....Roll your great green eyes over my grains!

(Everyone reacts to her suggestive delivery.)

MRS. VAN TASSEL

Rich wheels of wheat, rolls of rye, baguettes of buckwheat, and crunchy, colorful Indian corn with its golden ears peeping from leafy coverts holding out the promise of cakes and hasty pudding; and the yellow pumpkins lying beneath them, turning up their fair round bellies to the sun, and giving ample prospects of the most luxurious of pies. My orchards are simply burthened with ruddy fruit! On all sides, behold a vast store of apples, some hanging in oppressive opulence, some gathered into baskets and barrels, others heaped up in rich piles soon to be pressed into spiced hot cider! Breathe in the odor of the beehive, anticipate the sweet flavor of dainty slapjacks, well buttered and garnished with honey or treacle, by the delicate little dimpled hand of our own daughter, Katrina.

(Another round of oohs and ahhs from the revelers.)

ICHABOD

But now our minds are being fed with many "tart thoughts" and "sugared suppositions".

MRS. VAN TASSEL

And for the sweet tooth, just you dwell upon the ample charms of a genuine Dutch country tea table...Such heaped-up platters of cakes of various and almost indescribable kinds, known only to experienced Dutch housewives! There is the doughty doughnut, the crisp and crumbling cruller,

BROUWER

...sweet cakes and shortcakes,

HILDA

...ginger cakes and honey cakes,

DOFFUE

...and the whole family of cakes.

MRS. VAN TASSEL

...and then there are apple pies,

BALTUS

...and peach pies and pumpkin pies,

NICHOLAUS

...besides slices of ham and smoked beef;

MRS. VEDDER

and moreover delectable dishes of preserved plums,

MRS. VAN RIPPER

...and peaches, and pears and quinces,

(Peter Vanderdonk enters from kitchen with more steaming food on a tray)

VANDERDONK

...not to mention broiled shad and roasted chickens!

(All cheer and dig in.)

VAN RIPPER

...together with bowls of milk and cream,

ICHABOD

...all mingled higgledy-piggledy!

MRS. VAN TASSEL

…pretty much as I have enumerated them, with the motherly teapot sending up its clouds of vapor from the midst - Heaven bless the mark!

ALL

HEAVEN BLESS THE MARK!!

BALTUS

And now, shall we continue the night's revels as we are wont?! The sound of music from the common room summons us to dance! *(cheers)* Let us not see a limb nor fiber about you but is not in motion! No idle feet here! Dancers! Dancers!

(The dance begins. It should be beautifully choreographed beginning with the following pairs: Baltus and Mrs. Van Tassel, Brom Bones and Katrina, Mr. and Mrs. Van Ripper, MR. and Mrs. Vedder, Doffue Martling and his niece Hilda. Partners may be exchanged throughout depending on the choreography. Ichabod ends up with Katrina much to the chagrin of Brom Bones. Ichabod's dance becomes a crazy jig. All watch with amusement and amazement at how energetic yet truly ridiculous he is. The dance comes to an end. All applaud and bow or curtsey respectively to their partners.)

BALTUS

Excellent! Excellent! You would have thought Saint Vitus himself, that blessed patron of the dance, was figuring before us in person. At this time, those who desire it may retire to the piazza where we shall smoke our pipes, drink mulled wine, dole out wild and wonderful legends and spin yarns of ghosts and apparitions. Our chief tale tonight will be that favorite spectre of Sleepy Hollow, THE HEADLESS HORSEMAN, who has been heard several times of late, patrolling the country and tethering his horse nightly among the graves in the churchyard! To the piazza!

Scene 6. "War Stories"

(The men are on the Van Tassel piazza, while the women are gathered in the foreground in a clearing in front of the Van Tassel house. While the men tell stories of war, the women interject what really happened. This dialogue should be done in alternating fashion with the men oblivious to the wives words and the wives oblivious to the men's. Both groups are telling stories in different areas yet simultaneously.)

MRS. VAN TASSEL

I can just hear them now. Filling Master Crane's head with pure fiction!

(Ladies agree)

VAN TASSEL

…You see, Mynheer Crane, this neighborhood, at the time of which I am speaking, was one of those highly favored places which abound with chronicle and great men…

GARDINIER

They always make themselves the heroes of every exploit!

(Ladies agree)

BROUWER

…The British and American line had run near it during the war; it had therefore been the scene of marauding, and infested with refugees, cowboys, and all kinds of border chivalry…

MRS. VAN RIPPER

At which, our husbands were the first to lock up our doors and bolt the windows!

(Ladies giggle)

VAN RIPPER

…and I had nearly taken the British frigate with an old iron nine-pounder from a mud breastwork, only that my gun burst at the sixth discharge!…

(The men ooh and ah at the story, while the women see it a different way.)

MRS. VAN RIPPER

…He was so frightened, in fact, that upon hearing the British were coming he pulled the trigger prematurely and alerted the enemy to his regiment's location…

(The ladies fall into great laughter.)

VEDDER

…I, in the Battle of White Plains, being an excellent master of defense, parried a musket ball with a small sword, insomuch that I absolutely felt it whiz round the blade, and glance off at the hilt!…

(The men really excited at this one.)

MRS. VEDDER

…Master of the blade? Yes, he could use a paring knife very well. He was the regiment's cook and could chop carrots, onions, and peppers like no one else!…

(Ladies all burst into hysterical laughter.)

VEDDER

…In proof of which, I am ready at any time to show the sword with the hilt a little bent.…

MRS. VEDDER

…The only cause of his bent sword was getting it caught between his scabbard and a door jam!…

(More laughter)

VAN BRUNT

Enough war stories! I'm sure what Mynheer Crane would prefer to hear are stories of the Hessian of the Hollow...

ICHABOD

I'm well acquainted with the spirit soldier, if you'd rather...

VAN BRUNT

The galloping Hessian is the apparition, no doubt, of an arrant jockey who, believing his killer amongst the people of Sleepy Hollow, rides on a mission of vengeance. Perhaps Mynheer Crane fought in the war... he's certainly old enough to have done so. Is that why you've come to town, Crane? Is it fate that brought you and the Hessian together? Are you the man who beheaded the soldier? Is it you, he seeks? The blade of a saber clutched in his boney gripe? I once encountered the phantom. On returning one night from the neighboring village of Sing Sing, I had been overtaken by the midnight trooper. He had offered to race with him for a bowl of punch, and should have won it too, but Daredevil beat the goblin horse all hollow. And just as we came to the church bridge, the spectre turned into a skeleton, and bolted away over the treetops with a clap of thunder and a flash of fire.

(Crane withdraws his pocket watch.)

ICHABOD

Well, just look at the time! I really should be going. I'll just find Miss Katrina and perhaps she'll want to take a nice midnight stroll.

VAN BRUNT

Be careful, Schoolmaster. The Hollow isn't safe after dark.

ICHABOD

Yes, well,...your concern for my health, Brom Bones, gives one pause.

(A little music and all guests exit. Ichabod sees Katrina at a punch bowl and joins her. Brom Bones soon follows and joins the two. During Crayon's speech, Katrina is seen speaking to the two of them. She returns the book Ichabod gave her and takes Bones arm. They exit.)

CRAYON

The revel now gradually broke up. Ichabod only lingered behind, according to the custom of country lovers, to have a tete-a-tete with the heiress, fully convinced that he was now on the high road to success. What passed at this interview I will not pretend to say, for in fact I do not know. Something, however, I fear me, must have gone wrong for he certainly sallied forth with an air quite desolate and chopfallen...

(Ichabod procures his journal and quill.)

ICHABOD

"Thursday, October 31st, in the year of our Lord, seventeen hundred and ninety-five. It is now past midnight and I am overcome with a plague of melancholia. For my path has been crossed by a being that causes more perplexity to mortal man than ghosts, goblins, and the whole race of witches put together, and that is...a woman!

KNICKERBOCKER

Ichabod stole forth with the air of one who had been sacking a hen roost rather than a fair lady's heart. *(Crane exits to go to his horse offstage where an equestrian should be waiting to assist the actor in mounting.)* He went straight to the stable, without looking to the right or left to notice the scene of rural wealth, on which he had so often gloated.

CRAYON

Oh, these women! These women! Could that girl have been playing off any of her coquettish tricks? Was her encouragement of the poor pedagogue all a mere sham to secure her conquest of his rival?

KNICKBOCKER

Heaven only knows, not I! Once he had reached the stable, with several hearty cuffs and kicks he roused his steed most uncourteously from the comfortable quarters in which he was soundly sleeping, dreaming of mountains of corn and oats, and whole valleys of timothy and clover. Ichabod rode Gunpowder into the dead hush of midnight.

(Crane enters on horseback, whistling nervously. He arrives at center stage.)

ICHABOD

It is the very witching time of night that I, Ichabod Crane, heavy-hearted and crestfallen, pursue my travel homeward. All those stories of ghosts and goblins come crowding now upon my recollection. The night grows darker and darker. The stars seem to sink deeper in the sky and driving clouds hide them from my sight. I have never felt more lonely and dismal.

(The three apparitions materialize in clouds of smoke and ghoulish green under-lighting, upstage of Crane. They begin moaning direfully. Crane hears but does not see them yet. In fear, he shouts:)

ICHABOD

Angels and ministers of grace defend us! Come, Gunpowder!

(Crane kicks his horse and leads him off-stage and out of sight. Lights momentarily fade on the apparitions, hiding them in darkness.)

CRAYON

And with that, the panic of the steed had given his unskillful rider a jerk and a jolt which whipped the man to and fro in a frenzy. The girths of the saddle gave way, and he felt it slipping from under him. He seized it by the pommel and endeavoured to hold it firm, but in vain; He had just time to save himself by clasping old Gunpowder around the neck when the animal came to a stand with a suddenness that sent his rider sprawling over his head, and onto the earth.

KNICKERBOCKER

Gunpowder took off into the night, leaving the schoolmaster without a horse on which to make it home. *(Crane re-enters, this time on foot and carrying Gunpowder's saddle at his side)* The pedagogue ventured into the dark wood in search of his steed.

(Knickerbocker exits.)

ICHABOD

Gunpowder!

CRAYON

In the center of the clearing stood an enormous tree, which towered like a giant above all the other trees of the neighborhood and formed a kind of landmark. It was universally known by the name of "Major Andre's Tree". Unbeknownst to Crane, he was approaching the very place where many of the scenes of the ghost stories had been laid.

(Crayon exits.)

ICHABOD

Gunpowder! Come here, boy!

(Attempts to whistle the horse back)

Mynheer Van Ripper will be awfully perturbed if I return with your reigns and no horse underneath...GUNPOWDER!!! *(He sees something. Light intensifies on the Snow Maiden of Raven Rock. To himself now.)* In the dank mist of the forests fog, I behold a thing white, mysterious, floating upon the air? No, it is simply some shrub covered with snow and like a sheeted spectre, tricks the reason of mine eyes! Avaunt and quit my sight, foul foliage!

SNOW MAIDEN

*(Suddenly screams in agony. Then speaks to
Crane as if from a deep, dark crypt.)*

Ichabod Crane! 'Tis I, the Snow Maiden of Raven Rock. Hear my heart-broken voice. Look upon my skeletal visage frozen with a final countenance of terror, tears of ice splintered long ago in the bitter wind that stole my life. Caress my cracked and lesioned skin. Run your fingers through my matted hair, encrusted with frosty nests of sleeping grubs. Hold my stiffened sinew and brittle bones, kiss my leathery lips, and taste the sweet death of my breath, tainted with the stench of rotted flesh. Touch my arms and legs, feel my longing for love. Bloodless now and corrupt, my corse has withered with the years. I, a victim of winter's cruelty. Surely, *you* see the beauty in my hideousness. Come, Ichabod, make love to me, take my hand and come with us! Share with us our eternal home in Hell. Die with me, lie with me in my cold, cold crypt of ice!

> The horseman dealt his head a blow -
> His bones fell fast, a bloody heap.
> Maiden's hands emerged from snow,
> and pulled her lover down six feet deep!

ICHABOD

No!!!!!!! It cannot be! You are not real! It is no frost-bitten hag I see! No white witch I hear! This descent into madness is the issue of my own thoughts!

(Crane turns away and takes cover behind Major André's tree.)

Where am I now? Could this be the tree of Major Andre?

(Backing away from it now.)

It's limbs, gnarled and fantastic, twisting down almost to the earth and rising again into the air! Now gaze I narrowly upon a second ghostly form in white, hanging in its midst!

(Music builds in anticipation of the impending horror. Lights gradually intensify, illuminating the figure. It is now very clearly obvious that it is the still and lifeless form of Major Andre hanging from a noose.)

89

<u>ICHABOD</u>

My senses further betray me. It is no apparition! The tree has merely been scathed by lightning and the white wood laid bare.

(In an instant the corpse springs to life. Andre jerks his head in the direction of the pedagogue, opens his possessed, colorless eyes, darting them directly at Crane. Andre lets loose with a terrifying scream. Crane screams and hides his eyes from the horrifying visage. The Snow Maiden and Starkenfaust laugh maniacally.)

<u>MAJOR ANDRE</u>

FOOL! Dare you doubt our existence and turn your eyes from the truths of death?! Mark this tree well, Pedagogue! For my tragical story is carved into its very trunk with tales of strange sights and doleful lamentations. Feast upon my horrible visage! Regard my corrupt corpse, decaying in the wood, worm-infested and strung up in this mighty arbor where I have been left forever to rot in history! Hear my moans, Ichabod Crane,...*(Demonstrates a chilling moan)* as they blast forth, sweeping sharply through bristles and dry branches. Damned be your arrogance for entering this cursed ground! Let fear become your master, for...

> as your bones clatter
> and your teeth chatter,
> your knees will rattle
> against your saddle!

(The three apparitions howl in pain to further frighten Crane. Andre then expels a ghastly death rattle, closes his eyes and returns to his lifeless form. Underlighting on Starkenfaust rises to an eerie green, he speaks.)

<u>STARKENFAUST</u>

Mark me, Crane...lend a careful ear to my words. For I, Herman Von Starkenfaust am that very horseman without a skull. Hessian of Germany, commissioned by the British to fight in the great war. You see me now as I was in life. Regard my head firmly affixed upon strong shoulders and head my words...your only chance of survival in this wood from my demonic incarnation is the bridge. To pass the bridge is the severest trial. For when I ride headless, my horse is fast and my aim, expert. But once you cross, you have 'scaped with your life. My horse does not follow that which reaches the other side. Pray I don't dismount and pursue you on foot. For many have crossed the haunted stream never to return. Fearful are the feelings of every schoolboy who passes it alone after dark. Beware my headless form, Ichabod Crane, lest it creep up from behind and take you down, down to dusty death!

He that supper for is dight,
He lyes full cold, I trow, this night!
Yestreen to chamber I him led,
This night Grey-Steel has made his bed.

(Starkenfaust wails as a ghost. He senses the awakening of the "undead")

THREE APPARITIONS

Behold you now the souls of those departed from this world. Churchyards yawn and clandestine graves gape wide to release these Hell-bound hearts of the undead. How they stir from charnel beds and tear themselves loose from their eternal inferno. They awake disturbed, as you tread upon this cursed ground beneath which they once slept!

ICHABOD

Yet is there more?

(From out of trap doors, secret hovels and shallow graves, boney hands begin to tear away at their confinements as if awakening from a sleep of several hundred years. Corpses, the "undead" begin to claw their way out)

ICHABOD

The trees of the grove now seem to surround me, their limbs gnarled and twisted, and take on the personification of those inhabitants of Sleepy Hollow!...They are not trees! They are the waking dead! The damned, burst forth from yawning graveyards and risen to cast a warning! SPEAK, YOU TERRORS OF THE NIGHT! SPEAK!

Christopher Cook

(During the monologue above, the "undead" continue to drag and hobble themselves ever so slowly, closer to Ichabod Crane. They moan and groan as if struggling with the half-living, half-dead state of their physiology. Crane is all this time, rooted to the spot in paralyzing fear. Many of the corpses appear to be falling apart, dropping limbs and dried-up vital organs along the way. Creepy music swells underneath while the three apparitions impart the following warning in verse.)

<u>THREE APPARITIONS</u>

Beware the headless horseman,
On a nightly quest he rides.
To avenge his gruesome murder,
In the darkest wood he hides.

He's coming for you at a quarter to two.
Ride fast, you may survive.
But if you tarry for the weight you carry,
You'll no more be seen alive!

Clop, clop, clop,
His horse will never stop!

Chop, chop, chop,
His blade is sure to lop,

The scalp of your head,
The nape of your neck,
The mass above your chest.

You'll bleed bright red,
He'll leave you for dead,
Your corpse, there laid to rest.

Closer and closer,
You can hear the goblin's cape,
Closer and closer,
You're his, there's no escape!

92

He's on you now, he has you now!
You pray it's just a dream.

But your mind is sound,
Don't turn around.
All that's left to do is scream!

(The "undead" are now upon Crane and have closed in on him close enough to grab him. They reach out to engulf him in the center of their circle. Just as it appears he is doomed, the neighing of Ichabod's horse is heard in the distance.)

ICHABOD

GUN-POWDER!!!!!!

(Ichabod flees the scene, running backstage to once again mount the horse. The corpses do not follow him. As music continues, the three apparitions wave their arms, beckoning the "undead" back into their hovels and graves. They creep and crawl back to the Hell from which they came. The apparitions also vanish into fog and nothingness. Slightly overlapping the exit of the dead, Crane re-enters on horseback.)

ICHABOD

I behold something huge, misshapen, black and towering.

It stirs not but seems to gather up in the gloom,

Like some gigantic monster ready to spring upon me,

Hairs rise up upon my head with terror,

What is to be done?

To turn and fly is now too late!

What chance is there of escaping ghost or goblin

If such it is can ride upon the wings of the wind?

WHO ARE YOU?

WHO ARE YOU?

The shadowy object of alarm is now in motion --

(The Headless Horseman appears at the crest of the stage left hill. He carries at his side, holding by the hair, his freshly-severed head. Blood streams from the neck. The Hessian on horseback stands majestically and statuesque. Music has reached a crescendo.)

And though night is dark and dismal.

I see the creature, mysterious and appalling!

It is now fearfully accounted for!

The figure, gigantic in height, muffled in cloak -

Is to my horror-struck soul, HEAD-LESS!

Scene 7. "The Headless Horseman"

If I can but reach that bridge, I am safe! Run, Gunpowder, Run! For the goblin will surely hurl his severed head!

(Crane and his horse take off galloping toward the bridge, they cross it and continue to ride off into the distance. The Horseman and his steed, as though "sniffing-out" the center stage where Crane was, make several turns center, stand for a moment, cross the bridge and ride up onto a hill at stage left, to take one last "look". They descend the hill and then take-off in the direction of Ichabod Crane's chosen path. Both riders now have ridden off into the darkness of the night.)

EPILOGUE

(The chaos from the encounter with the Headless Horseman dies out and morning music and lighting fade in. Enter the Van Tassels and Mr. and Mrs. Van Ripper. All enter with lit lanterns.)

VAN TASSEL

Good Morning, Mynheer.

VAN RIPPER

Morning, Van Tassel.

VAN TASSEL

Any word?

VAN RIPPER

None.

MRS. VAN RIPPER

Mynheer Crane did not make an appearance at breakfast.

VAN RIPPER

An inquiry has been set on foot and the Constable has called for a diligent investigation. His volunteers are arriving just now.

(Enter Vanderdonk, Van Houten and Vedders.)

VAN HOUTEN

The horse was found but no saddle.

VANDERDONK

The bridle and reins on the grass at the horses feet.

(Enter Sleepy Hollow Boys and others)

VAN BRUNT

We checked the schoolhouse but no Mynheer Crane.

MRS. VEDDER

We searched the brook, but the body of the schoolmaster was not to be discovered.

BROUWER

He's not in the church. But on one part of the road leading to the graveyard we found the saddle trampled in the dirt,...

DOFFUE

Mynheer Crane's hat, and close beside it a shattered pumpkin.

KATRINA

He's gone.

VAN TASSEL

Hans Van Ripper, you're the executor of Crane's estate. What has he left behind?

VAN RIPPER

I've examined the bundle which contained all
his worldly effects, and I found...

(Reading from a list)

"Two shirts and a half, two neck stocks, two pair of worsted stockings, an old pair of corduroy pantaloons, a rusty razor, a much dog-eared book of psalm tunes, and a broken pitch pipe." These items I'll divvy among those in need. As to the books and furniture of the schoolhouse, they belong to the community. However, the books on music, fortune-telling, dreams, this Cotton Mather's History of Witchcraft - I shall consign all these books to the flames from whence they came. From this time forward I am determined to send my children no more to school. I never knew any good come of this same reading and writing anyway.

MRS. VAN RIPPER

What's happened to the man?

MRS. VAN TASSEL

It's obvious he flew from the place from a broken heart.

VAN BRUNT

He was presumptuous. And that led to his demise.

MRS. VEDDER

He was no doubt spirited away by supernatural means.

GARDINIER

Abducted by the galloping Hessian and cast into the underworld.

BROUWER

Poor damned soul. We must continue our search that he may be interred in consecrated ground.

(All freeze in position, except Knickerbocker who crosses center.)

KNICKERBOCKER

As he was a bachelor and in nobody's debt no one troubled his head about the schoolmaster anymore. Brom Bones, shortly after his rival's disappearance, conducted the blooming Katrina in triumph to the alter. He was observed to look exceedingly knowing whenever the story of Ichabod was related which led some to suspect that he knew more about the matter than he chose to tell. The schoolhouse, being deserted, soon fell to decay and was reported to be haunted by the ghost of the unfortunate pedagogue. The inhabitants of Tarry Town, loitering homeward of a still autumn evening, often fancy his voice at a distance, chanting a melancholy psalm tune among the tranquil solitudes of Sleepy Hollow.

(Ensemble moves in slow motion with lanterns. Into Tableau. Lights. Fog. Music swells.)

END OF PLAY

NOTES TO THE DIRECTOR

Every effort should be made to maintain the integrity of Washington Irving's original tale. Where logical, I have used as many of Irving's own words as possible. In other places, I have had to create dialogue which would preserve the tenor of the established circa and characterizations. Through artistic license, I have woven into the play three conventions unique to this adaptation, yet textually supported; a swordfight between Crane and Van Brunt, the appearance of three apparitions whose names are found in Irving's writing, though not perhaps full-fledged characters in *The Legend of Sleepy Hollow*, and the "walking dead", who are, in essence, the personification of the evil that Ichabod Crane perceives to be haunting him in the dark wood.

Blades used in the swordfight should be rapiers indigenous to the established time and place. The choreography should depict Ichabod Crane as inept in his attempt at swordplay and Brom Bones as the clear expert. Since the combat ends act one, it is a good idea to allow it to be as comical, fast-paced, and exciting as possible. Incidentally, this published adaptation is the *first* and *only* to feature a sword fight. There is not, of course, any fighting with swords from Irving's novella, and as there is no sword fight in his story, any other adaptation forthcoming using such a convention is simply plagiarizing the Cook version.

When the undead appear, the actors should be directed to stay within the world of the play and not to break the so-called "4th wall" by interacting with the audience. There is a tendency on the actor's part to reach out and startle the children on the front row. This would be a mistake. Allowing the corpses to do this reveals their actual impotency by exposing the limits of their malevolence. Much more effective is to have the zombies respect the "4th wall", some of them getting uncomfortably close to the nearest audience members, but never actually acknowledging them. In this manner, the world of the play is preserved and the undead never lay all their proverbial cards out on the table. In the end, this will illicit a greater sense of dread. To an audience, the unknown is always more frightening than the known.

The music chosen should be classical in nature to reflect the period of the piece. The director should carefully select the music so as not to play anything so familiar to a contemporary audience that they are taken out of the 18th - Century world the designers have worked so hard to create.

Finally, the actors playing Knickerbocker and Crayon should be required to learn their lines word-perfect. There has been a tendency in past performances for the narrators to rely solely upon a hand-held desk with their lines "discreetly" pasted in the spine. When that precedent is set, deliberately or not, the lines seem never to be actually committed to memory. And opening night you will have actors with good intentions yet poor results. The narration will all be read. It is certain. It is of course perfectly acceptable for the narrators to carry quills and parchment. But the roles of Knickerbocker and Crayon were never intended to be read. Rather they must be spoken. They are telling the story and writing it as the tale unfolds. This keeps the narrative alive and active. Break-a-leg!

A GLOSSARY OF SELECT TERMS

Amsterdam: located in Holland, the capital and largest city of the Netherlands: significant port and financial center widely known for its diamond industry.

Andre, Major: John (1750-80), British soldier. He successfully negotiated with Benedict Arnold for the betrayal of West Point to the British 1779-80. Captured while returning from West Point, he was tried and hanged as a spy.

beset: (adj.) the condition of being surrounded on all sides.

birch: (n.) a tree providing hard, close-grained wood.

boorish: (adj.) characterized by clumsy manners and little refinement; rude.

burthened: (adj.) replete with or endowed with.

bustle: (n.) any rambunctious or lively activity.

capacious: (adj.) having a lot of room or space.

cavalier: (n.) a very gallant gentleman; a knight.

cognomen: (n.) scientific name or classification of any genus or species.

conning: (v.) the act of poring over or studying something with careful diligence and attention to detail.

coquette: (n.) a woman who flirts.

corpus: (n.) (lat.) the body or physical part of a human being.

countenance: (n.) the face as an indication of mood or character, bearing or expression that would suggest approval or sanction.

crane: (n.) a bird whose bodily structure is adaptable to foraging: usually in waterways and swamplands. Inhabitants nearest the Hudson River would most likely be familiar with the Yellow Rail which nests in prairie marshes in the northeastern-most territories of the United States.

direful: (adj.) dreadful or terrible in consequence.

double-up: (v.) cause to bend over or curl up with pain.

drones: (n.) (pl.) male bees which do no work yet are capable of fertilizing a queen.

eel pot: (n.) a device for trapping eels and preventing their escape.

emancipation: (n.) liberation; having been set free from bondage.

frolic: (n.) merriness; a romp or a playful, carefree occasion

gambols: (n.) (pl.) an action of frolic, skipping, or leaping about in play.

gamecock: (n.) a rooster bred and trained for cockfighting: also called game foul.

goblin: (n.) in folklore, an ugly, grotesque creature said to be mischievous and evil.

grievous: (adj.) causing grief, sorrow, anguish, or pain; causing physical suffering.

Hessian: (n.) military troopers indigenous to the state in western Germany known as Hesse: its capital is Wiesbaden. These soldiers were often commissioned by British armies for the reinforcement of their troops during the Revolutionary War.

hubbub: (n.) a state of confusion, an uproar.

Hudson, Hendrick: (1565-1611) English explorer: he discovered the North American bay, river, and straight that bear his name. In 1610, he attempted to winter in Hudson Bay, but his crew mutinied and set Hudson and a few companies adrift, never to be seen again.

idiosyncratic: (adj.) having peculiar behavior. To a particular personality trait.

imbibe: (v.) to drink; to take in.

impunity: (n.) exemption from punishment.

knights-errant of yore: (n.) (pl.) soldiers who served a monarch as far back as the middle ages.

laud: (n.) late middle English: from old French *laude*, meaning praise.

Mather, Cotton: (1663-1728) American minister and writer; son of Increase Mather. Noted for his political writings, he sponsored the Massachusetts charter in 1691 and is thought to have influenced the events that lead to the Salem witch trials in 1692.

mynheer: a contraction of the Dutch, *Myn Heer*, a title of respect reserved for the adult male gentleman.

onerous: (adj.) late middle English: of a task, duty, or responsibility involving an amount of effort and difficulty that is oppressively burdensome.

parson: (n.) a pastor or clergyman.

partridge: (n.) a plump or stout-bodied game bird.

pedagogue: (n.) one who teaches or is in the profession of educating or instructing.

peradventure: (n.) late middle English: uncertainty or doubt as to whether something is the case.

perambulations: (n.) (pl.) late middle English: walks or travels through or around a place or area, especially for pleasure and in a leisurely way.

perplexity: (n.) a confusion or state of being confused; a complication.

petticoat: (n.) a woman's skirt-like garment worn as an underskirt.

piazza: (n.) a public square or an open area typically in an Italian town or city.

pique: (v.) mid 16th -century: to pride oneself.

portentous: (adj.) done in a pompously or overly solemn manner so as to impress.

potentate: (n.) late middle English: a monarch or ruler, particularly an autocratic one.

propensity: (n.) late 16th -century: an inclination or natural tendency to behave in a particular manner.

psalmody: (n.) the practice of singing sacred hymns, taken from the book of Psalms in the Old Testament.

purport: (v.) to give the appearance of intending; to imply usually with the intent to deceive.

purveyor: (n.) one in the business of providing or supplying specific items or services.

quavers: (n.) (pl.) late middle English: a shake or tremble in a person's voice. Most likely derived from an old English word related to *quake*. The noun was first recorded in the mid 16ᵗʰ -century as a musical term.

quilting frolic: (n.) a festive occasion to complete or display recently sewn

racketing: (v.) mid 16ᵗʰ -century: making a loud, unpleasant noise: perhaps initiative of clattering.

repose: (n.) the act of being at rest.

reverie: (n.) early 17ᵗʰ -century: a state of being pleasantly lost in one's thoughts; a daydream.

roistering: (v.) late 16ᵗʰ -century: enjoying oneself or celebrating in a noisy or boisterous way.

ruddy: (adj.) being red in color or hue.

scourings: (n.) (pl.) late middle English: rapid movements in a particular direction, especially in search or in pursuit of someone or something.

single combat: (n.) an act of physical conflict between two individuals; includes fighting with or without weaponry.

snipe: (n.) a bird with a long bill which lives in marshy places.

sojourned: (v.) middle English: stayed temporarily.

spectral: (adj.) early 18ᵗʰ -century: of or like a ghost.

stripling: (n.) middle English: a young man.

strudel: (n.) German origin: a confection of thin pastry rolled up and around a fruit filling, then baked.

sullen: (adj.) ill-humored, melancholy; gloomy; depressing.

sumptuous: (adj.) late middle English: made or produced at great cost

tarry: (v.) to linger, delay, or hesitate.

Tartar: (n.) a member of the combined forces of central Asian peoples, including Monguls and Turks, who under the leadership of Genghis Kahn conquered Asian and easern Europe in the early 13th century.

trumpery: (n.) late middle English: attractive articles of little value or use.

whirligig: (n.) late middle English: a toy that spins around, for example, a top or pinwheel

wight: (n.) Old English: a person of a specified kind. A thing or creature.

withe: (n.) a tough, flexible branch of an osier or other willow, used for tying, binding, or basketry.

THE PLAYWRIGHT

Christopher Cook holds an MFA in Directing from the Theatre Conservatory of Roosevelt University in Chicago, Illinois and a BA in Drama from Winthrop College. He is the Artistic Director of High Voltage Theatre in Columbia, South Carolina where he has directed *COWBOY MOUTH, RESERVOIR DOGS, SUNDANCE, BREAKING LEGS,* and *THE LEGEND OF SLEEPY HOLLOW* ('02, '03, '04, '07). Chicago directing credits include *LOOT, BACK BOG BEAST BAIT, NOMADS,* and co-direction of *RESERVOIR DOGS* with Azusa Productions.

A veteran actor of over 80 productions, Mr. Cook has worked with the South Carolina Shakespeare Company, having assayed the title role in *CYRANO DE BERGERAC* to critical acclaim, Don John in *MUCH ADO ABOUT NOTHING* as well as taken the director's chair for *OTHELLO,* subsequently named by *The State* as one of the 10 best Columbia productions of 2001. Other roles of note include, Malvolio, Jacques, Mercutio, Hector, Tybalt, Macduff, Banquo and Peter Quince.

Regional theatre credits include New York City's National Theatre of the Performing Arts, Broadway's Town Hall, the Kennedy Center in Washington, DC, The Civic Center in San Francisco, California, Chicago Shakespeare Theater, the New Jersey Shakespeare Festival, the Colorado Shakespeare Festival, and the Charlotte Shakespeare Company. An Irene Ryan Award and Joseph Jefferson Award nominee, he is Columbia's pre-eminent Fight Choreographer to the stage and is an active member of both the Society of American Fight Directors as well as the International Brotherhood of Magicians.

Mr. Cook is a master professor of the Theatre Arts and has served on the faculties of Newberry College, Limestone College, and Midlands Technical College. Mr. Cook is privileged to have worked closely with actor Ed Dennehy, *Sex and the City's* Kristin Davis, *My Girl's* Anna Chlumsky, and Pulitzer Prize-winner Beth Henley. He is happily married with one daughter and currently resides in Columbia, South Carolina, his hometown.

NOTES

NOTES

NOTES

NOTES

NOTES

Made in the USA
Middletown, DE
08 July 2015